About the authors

Herb Lester Associates publish city guides with style. Their beautifully designed fold-out maps sidestep famous landmarks and faddy new attractions in favour of a more beguiling world.

Their carefully researched and highly opinionated guides highlight the best of new and old; book and record shops, cobblers, museums and galleries, theirs is a quest for good quality things to see, eat, drink and do. With a Herb Lester guide you will not be left wanting; sustenance, expertly poured drinks and splendid entertainment – as well as a gentlemen's hat shop, a purveyor of preserved fish and a vintage furniture shop for life's little emergencies, may be around the next corner.

www.herblester.com

A London Pub for Every Occasion

161 of the usual and unusual

Brought to you by
Herb Lester Associates

Edited by Ben Olins & Jane Smillie
Written by Ben Olins
Illustrations by Anna Hurley

EBURY
PRESS

3 5 7 9 10 8 6 4 2

Published in 2014 by Ebury Press, an imprint of Ebury Publishing,
A Random House Group Company

Text © Herb Lester Associates 2014
Illustrations by Anna Hurley © Herb Lester Associates 2014

The Random House Group Limited Reg. No. 954009

Addresses for companies within the Random House Group can be found at
www.randomhouse.co.uk

A CIP catalogue record for this book is available from the British Library

The Random House Group Limited supports the Forest Stewardship
Council® (FSC®), the leading international forest-certification organisation.
Our books carrying the FSC label are printed on FSC®-certified paper.
FSC is the only forest-certification scheme supported by the leading
environmental organisations, including Greenpeace. Our paper procurement
policy can be found at www.randomhouse.co.uk/environment

To buy books by your favourite authors and register for offers visit
www.randomhouse.co.uk

Printed and bound in Italy by L.E.G.O. S.p.A.

ISBN 978 0 091 95827 5

Contents

Introduction

Those of us who like pubs already have our favourites, places we barely consider for being so woven into our lives. Away from routine and familiar territory things get more confusing, which is where our guide comes in. It is our intention to introduce the reader to new pubs and to encourage a fresh look at old favourites.

We have divided the book into chapters based on scenarios: where to go when it's sunny, or wet, to meet before a show, after a trip to the Natural History Museum, before boarding a train at St Pancras, when you're alone, or when you have friends you can't be bothered to chat with. Then there are pubs for moods, interests and atmosphere: beautiful old pubs, pubs with wonderful beer and a handful that fill you with such a feeling of bonhomie you can't bear to leave them.

In creating any guide to London, the city's vastness is an issue to be grappled with. It's simply too big to do equal justice to all areas. We have weighted this guide to the centre, the part of the city in which all Londoners have an equal share, where friends from the south and north of the river meet on common ground. The east and parts of the north are also strongly represented, which is a reflection of a particularly vibrant (and highly competitive) pub culture rather than mere parochialism on our part.

We should confess our preference for pubs with real ale, real fires and little or no music; for friendly staff, dim light and a couple of animals roaming around. Equally, we struggle to enjoy pubs that have large TVs, blackboards with humorous sayings, or fashionably abbreviated names. This book's selections are based on dogged research filtered through the prejudices listed above. We have tried to be fair but, more important, we have tried to steer the reader to places we believe they'll appreciate for one reason or another.

Our research for this book took us to parts of London that we'd never been to before, it gave us the opportunity to revisit favourite pubs and to find new ones. We hope you enjoy using this guide as much as we did compiling it.

It's not too early is it?

Those whose jobs demand inhospitable hours are entitled to an after-work drink; for the rest of us, we pose the above question. Should you require a glass of beer with your bacon and eggs, read on.

Fox & Anchor

115 Charterhouse Street EC1M 6AA
Telephone: 020 7250 1300
Monday-Friday: 7am-11pm; Saturday: 8.30am-11pm;
Sunday: 8.30am-10pm
Transport: Barbican, Farringdon

Rescued from dereliction by the Malmaison hotel chain, this has become more than just a pub, with its own half-dozen rooms to rent upstairs and a strong emphasis on food. It's beautiful still – the tiles are particularly noteworthy – but the narrow layout can make it a squeeze at busy times, never more so than after tackling the City Boy breakfast. This gargantuan serving, which draws on nearby Smithfield meat market for inspiration, includes liver, kidney, steak, sausage, black and white puddings, bacon, eggs and sundry non-meat elements. And it's served with a pint of stout too. There are more modest options available, but no matter which you opt for, try to bag one of the private wooden booths in the back. Not only are they attractive, they're useful for a quick doze after your meal.

The Hope

94 Cowcross Street EC1M 6BH
Telephone: 020 7253 8525 (restaurant) or 020 7250 1442 (bar)
Monday-Friday: 6am-11pm; Saturday: 1pm–11pm
Transport: Farringdon

If the Fox & Anchor's reimagining of the old meat market pub for the modern consumer feels inauthentic, the experience here may be more to your taste. Modest in size, it has a handsome exterior, with central arched windows and doors continuing the pattern either side. Inside it's somewhat worn; maintained rather than cherished. Its regulars show evident surprise at new arrivals, but it's safe to assume that not much would shock the denizens of any pub that opens at 6am. Breakfasts – large, small or liquid – are served to shift workers, weary revellers, and anyone else in need.

The Market Porter

9 Stoney Street SE1 9AA
Telephone: 020 7407 2495
Monday-Friday: 6am-9am & 11am-11pm;
Saturday: 12noon-11pm; Sunday: 12noon-10.30pm
Transport: London Bridge

It's all about how you define breakfast, but if a pint and
a packet of dry roasted is what you require before the
school run, or indeed after a gruelling 2am start from your
smallholding to make a delivery to Borough Market, here's
where to go. For somewhere so intimately bound up with
London's best known food market, it's extraordinarily, even
refreshingly, basic – fish and chips is served sans samphire,
for example – but the beer range is good and this large
pub remains hugely popular, whatever the time of day.

Old Kings Head

28 Holywell Row EC2A 4JB
Telephone: 020 7426 0658
Monday-Friday: 8am-11pm; Saturday: 11am-11pm
Transport: Shoreditch High Street, Old Street

With no ancient market or all-night postal depot to service,
offering breakfast here is just canny business sense. On a
rat run from City Road to Great Eastern Street, dozens of
bleary-eyed workers stop in to pick up one of the particularly
good bacon sandwiches (just £2) on the way to the office.
You can eat in too; the menu includes eggs Benedict, granola,
pancakes and, of course, the full monty. With talk radio
burbling and the bustle of early morning deliveries and
cleaning, the atmosphere is nicely industrious, with tea and
coffee drinking far more evident than anything stronger.

Simpson's Tavern

Ball Court, 38½ Cornhill EC3V 9DR
Telephone: 020 7626 9985
Monday: 12noon-3pm; Tuesday-Friday: 8am-3pm
Transport: Bank

If breakfast in a tavern appeals, but perhaps without the aroma of last night's slops, at this remarkably unaltered 18th-century establishment you can tuck in to a full English (Cumberland sausage, bacon, black or white pudding, egg, mushrooms, tomato, baked beans and unlimited toast), porridge or simple poached eggs, and order your sharpener from the separate bar area. Of course, coffee and tea are also available, but it's nice to know the option's there for something stronger.

Because you wouldn't believe it otherwise

A selection of the eccentric, outlandish and unexpected; these are pubs you must see.

The Churchill Arms

119 Kensington Church Street W8 7LN
Telephone: 020 7727 4242
Monday-Wednesday: 11am-11pm;
Thursday-Saturday: 11am-12midnight;
Sunday: 12noon-10.30pm
Transport: High Street Kensington, Notting Hill Gate

In summer this pub's frontage peers out of foliage like
a highland cow through its fringe, only partially visible
through the greenery; it's not for nothing twice winner of
London in Bloom awards. Inside, all architectural features
are similarly obscured by the accumulation of *stuff*. Stuck to
walls or suspended from the ceiling are life-size cut-outs of
the Duke and Duchess of Cambridge, old radios, baskets,
an accordion and Sir Winston Churchill in old newspapers,
photos and sundry ephemera. A road sign points the way
to the bar and the gents. Head to the back and you find a
Thai restaurant occupying a similarly peculiar conservatory
area. It's contrived and it's showy, but not without charm.

The Nags Head

53 Kinnerton Street SW1X 8ED
Telephone: 020 7235 1135
Monday-Saturday: 11am-11pm; Sunday: 12noon-10.30pm
Transport: Knightsbridge

One of a rare breed of places that insists absolutely you enjoy
your own company or that of the person sitting next to you.
The main bar is low, disconcertingly so, and the loftier visitor
may feel like Gulliver on entering, with service somewhere
around thigh height and drinkers hunkered on low stools.
There's another room downstairs with a flagstone floor, its
walls and ceilings liberally covered with ephemera of numerous
eras; there are Edwardian seaside novelties, wooden ice skates,
swords, a saddle, a typewriter. For so smart a neighbourhood,
the crowd is pleasantly diverse.

The Sherlock Holmes

10-11 Northumberland Street WC2N 5DB
Telephone: 020 7930 2644
Sunday-Thursday: 11am-11pm;
Friday & Saturday: 11am-12midnight
Transport: Charing Cross, Embankment

Using props acquired from the Festival of Britain's tribute to Sherlock Holmes, in 1957 Whitbread assembled a room based on the study of 221b Baker Street on the first floor of a pub that may or may not be on the site Conan Doyle had in mind for the Northumberland Hotel. For the uninitiated, this is where Sir Henry Baskerville stayed in the story *The Hound of the Baskervilles*, when seeking assistance from Holmes regarding the matter of a family curse. Today the entire pub is filled with Sherlockiana; there's the head of a goofy-looking hound, a violin, Watson's pistol, and all over are stills from stage, TV and film versions. Not somewhere to linger perhaps, but a real curiosity. It's not easy to imagine the great detective enjoying one of their special offer mojitos, but as an observer of aberrant human behaviour, it's possible that Holmes would have been intrigued by this preposterous homage.

The Ship & Shovell

1-3 Craven Passage WC2N 5PH
Telephone: 020 7839 1311
Monday-Saturday: 11am-11pm
Transport: Charing Cross, Embankment

A single pub that masquerades as two, the buildings facing each other across a pedestrian passage, allowing a free flow from one to the other. Both facades are painted a cheerful shade of red, with matching barrels outside for the resting of drinks, and while neither is architecturally remarkable inside or out, they're comfortable and well-managed, and this arrangement is a one of a kind. It's worth noting that at quiet times the south building may be closed.

Wibbley Wobbley

Greenland Dock, off Rope Street SE16 7SZ
Telephone: 020 7232 2320
Monday–Saturday: 11am–11pm; Sunday: 12noon–10.30pm
Transport: Surrey Quays

As unpretentious as it is unlikely, this floating licensed premises is no flash in the plan; it has been moored here for 20 years and was in a nearby dock for 10 years before that. A pontoon floats alongside for outdoor seating and a weekend barbecue, but for all its wibbling and wobbling, this is a surprisingly normal pub. With no cellar and constant movement, cask ale is not an option.

Windsor Castle

27–29 Crawford Place W1H 4LJ
Telephone: 020 7723 4371
Monday–Saturday: 11am–11pm; Sunday: 12noon–10pm
Transport: Edgware Road

Despite what some guides may tell you, this is not a typical London pub. Not by a long shot. It is a bizarre and entirely contrived monument to, and arguably an example of, English eccentricity. It's cluttered with memorabilia relating to the royal family, the Second World War and largely forgotten stars of British TV. It's proved popular with esoteric clubs, a number of which hold gatherings here, most famously the Handlebar Club (est. 1947), on the first Friday of the month. You may take that as a warning.

When it's nice out

If the sun shines, even a patch of pavement feels like luxury. What follows are true delights, with river views or attractive gardens, and worth a journey.

The Bell & Crown

11–13 Thames Road W4 3PL
Telephone: 020 8994 4164
Monday-Saturday: 11am-11pm; Sunday: 12noon-10.30pm
Transport: Gunnersbury, Kew Bridge

A little closer to the bridge than The City Barge (below), it's a smarter, tidier pub than that one, albeit slightly less atmospheric. It would be churlish to sneer at it though, with a terrace overlooking the river, tables and a handy wall opposite, on which one can sit with legs dangling over the riverbank.

The City Barge

27 Strand-on-the-Green, W4 3PH
Telephone: 020 8994 2148
Daily: 11am-11pm
Transport: Gunnersbury, Kew Bridge

Just a short walk along the river from Kew Bridge, almost opposite Oliver's Island, a densely-wooded little outpost in the Thames' muddy waters. Inside it's on two levels, with open fires on each, but the downstairs feels older and more intimate. It's probably at its best in summer, when outside tables allow drinkers and an assortment of dogs to catch the last of the sun's warmth. The City Barge is also known for a brief appearance in The Beatles' movie *Help!*

The Dove

19 Upper Mall W6 9TA
Telephone: 020 8748 9474
Monday–Saturday: 11am–11pm; Sunday: 12noon–10.30pm
Transport: Hammersmith, Ravenscourt Park

On a clear day, to sit outside The Dove with a refreshing drink
and enjoy the view of the Thames and Hammersmith Bridge
is one of this city's great joys. Add a little sunshine and a few
bobbing vessels and it's hard not to feel some patriotic stirrings
– small wonder, then, that James Thomson was supposedly
inspired to write *Rule, Britannia!* on these premises. For all the
loveliness of the river, even in gloom The Dove has its charms.
A fire blazes in the tiny front bar, its flame reflected in brass-
topped tables, the woodwork is worn with use and softened
with coats of shining black paint – a scene of cosiness and
comfort, just yards from the terrors of the Great West Road.

Faltering Fullback

19 Perth Road N4 3HB
Telephone: 020 7272 5834
Monday-Thursday: 12noon-11.30pm;
Friday & Satuday: 12noon-12.30am;
Sunday: 12noon-11pm
Transport: Finsbury Park

A much-loved ivy-covered north London local, the interior is dense with *objets trouvés* – guitars, baskets, scarves and all manner of sporting paraphernalia. With what appears just a small space for a garden, you may wonder how it is that so many people seem to be heading for it and not turning back – the allure is an elaborate treehouse-like construction of several levels, which cleverly compensates for the relatively meagre footprint.

The Grapes

76 Narrow Street E14 8BP
Telephone: 020 7987 4396
Monday-Wednesday: 12noon-3.30pm & 5.30pm-11pm;
Thursday-Saturday: 12noon-11pm; Sunday: 12noon-10.30pm
Transport: Limehouse, Westferry

Modest in appearance, with a narrow front, hanging baskets and etched glass, it lacks the theme-bar feel of many other riverside inns. There's a gentle burble of good conversation as friends sit around tables enjoying each other's company. It's dark but not gloomy; glass-shaded lights emit a setting-sun glow and from the far end of the room comes daylight and the welcome sight of the Thames, which can also be viewed from a small deck with chairs. Dickens used it as the model for his hostelry the Six Jolly Fellowship-Porters in *Our Mutual Friend*, at which time it was a rough establishment 'of a dropsical appearance'. Today it is considerably gentrified, but still cosy, charming and welcoming.

The Lamb Tavern

10-12 Leadenhall Market EC3V 1LR
Telephone: 020 7626 2454
Monday-Friday: 11am-11pm
Transport: Bank, Fenchurch Street, Monument

As with most pubs in the City, the trick here is to avoid the crowds. In late morning and mid afternoon there's room to breathe and to absorb in peace a beautiful setting, amid the glass and iron of Leadenhall Market, a masterpiece of Victorian structural engineering and ornamentation. Sunshine may bring out the best in the market's livery, but there's some satisfaction to be had standing sheltered as rain drums on the glass canopy above. When the nights draw in, beneath The Lamb is Old Tom's Bar with glorious Victorian tiles, serving drinks from smaller breweries and distillers along with meat and cheese boards.

The Mayflower

117 Rotherhithe Street SE16 4NF
Telephone: 020 7237 4088
Monday-Saturday: 11am-11pm; Sunday: 12noon-10.30pm
Transport: Canada Water, Rotherhithe

A pub called The Shippe was on this site in 1620, when nearby the Pilgrim Fathers boarded the *Mayflower* and set sail for America. Had the current hostelry been open then, how different things might have turned out, as they decided to stay for just one more, admiring the view from the little jetty, listening to the water lapping, using one of the blankets thoughtfully provided for when the air turned chilly. Today the view takes in some of London's more regrettable architectural decisions, but there are still plenty of fine old buildings to admire. River aside, the interior is as dark and warm as you could wish for.

Roebuck

130 Richmond Hill TW10 6RN
Telephone: 020 8948 2329
Monday-Thursday: 12noon-11pm;
Friday & Saturday: 12noon-12midnight;
Sunday: 12noon-10.30pm
Transport: Richmond

There may be people who like to sit inside this perfectly
pleasant pub, but we've not met them. Its situation, on
top of the hill at Richmond, with views of the river and
surrounding countryside is remarkable, and while there's
not a garden as such, there is seating opposite which
makes it an ideal spot on warm, or at least sunny, days.

The Scarsdale Tavern

23a Edwardes Square W8 6HE
Telephone: 020 7937 1811
Monday-Saturday: 12noon-11pm; Sunday: 12noon-10.30pm
Transport: Earl's Court, High Street Kensington

On this beautiful Georgian square, with its three-acre
garden (residents only except for Open Garden Squares
Weekend), The Scarsdale is a more friendly and lived-in place
than one might expect. Inside, it's dimly-lit and rambling,
with two fireplaces and semi-private nooks. There's a food
section with open kitchen that's sectioned off by a wood
and stained glass partition, with a curtain for extra privacy.
The small terrace in the front feels sheltered and secluded.

Windsor Castle

114 Campden Hill Road W8 7AR
Telephone: 020 7243 8797
Monday-Saturday: 12noon-11pm; Sunday: 12noon-10.30pm
Transport: Holland Park, Notting Hill Gate

People come from far and wide for the Windsor Castle's garden, its high walls affording protection even on a brisk summer's day. In fact one can bypass the pub completely entering the garden by its own entrance on Peel Street. To do so would be to miss out on the creaky, sloping-floored interior, which has three discrete bars – Private, Campden and Sherry and a country feel quite out of character for its location. Despite this, the Windsor Castle is very much a modern affluent West London take on the pub, with an emphasis on food and, as such, it is as noted in *The New London Spy* in 1966, 'almost, but not quite, made totally impossible by the clientele who like to be seen there'.

Keep on the sunny side

The Anchor & Hope

15 High Hill Ferry E5 9HG
Telephone: 020 8806 1730
Monday-Thursday: 1pm-11pm;
Friday & Saturday: 12noon-11pm;
Sunday: 12noon-10.30pm
Transport: Clapton

The Blythe Hill Tavern

319 Stanstead Road SE23 1JB
Telephone: 020 8690 5176
Monday-Wednesday: 11am-11pm;
Thursday-Saturday: 11am-12midnight;
Sunday: 12noon-11pm
Transport: Catford

The Blue Anchor

13 Lower Mall W6 9DJ
Telephone: 020 8748 5774
Monday-Saturday: 12noon-11pm;
Sunday: 12noon-10.30pm
Transport: Hammersmith,
Ravenscourt Park

The Hermit's Cave

28 Camberwell Church Street
SE5 8QU
Monday-Wednesday: 12noon-12midnight;
Thursday-Saturday: 12noon-2am;
Sunday: 12noon-1am
Transport: Denmark Hill

When it's chilly

A warm pub is one of the consolations of the winter months.
A place to stay dry and huddle, protected from the elements.

The Angel

61-62 St Giles High Street WC2H 8LE
Telephone: 020 7240 2876
Monday-Saturday: 12noon–11pm; Sunday: 12noon–10.30pm
Transport: Tottenham Court Road

St Giles, once a notorious slum and today a small island amidst roaring traffic and vast construction sites, is undergoing yet another attempt at regeneration. Given the scale of construction, it may be that this 19th-century pub is all that survives of a still scrappy and shady part of the West End. As a winter bolthole, it's unbeatable, divided into three comfortable bars, two of which are connected by an interior tiled passageway, so that cool damp air bursts in with each new customer, a reminder of what one is taking shelter from.

The Bell

29 Bush Lane EC4R 0AN
Telephone: 0207 929 7772
Monday-Friday: 11am–10pm
Transport: Cannon Street, Monument

With its low ceiling, open fire, a menu that leans toward comforting old-fashioned doorstep sandwiches and a history that dates back to before the Great Fire, this is a very effective hiding place when the wind is whipping. Despite its age, it has an ersatz feel with copper pans hanging from the timbered ceiling, horse brasses on the wall and glowing Courage sign above the bar. Two wall-mounted TVs are a regrettable decision, but neither is particularly large or obtrusive.

Cutty Sark

4-6 Ballast Quay SE10 9PD
Telephone: 020 8858 3146
Monday-Saturday: 11am-11pm; Sunday: 12noon-10.30pm
Transport: Cutty Sark, Maze Hill

In the summer there's seating from which to contemplate the
O2, Canary Wharf and other follies yet to be completed across
the river, but perhaps it's even better on a wintry day, perched
by the fire. The interior is undeniably dark and warm with low
ceilings. Food appears to be the priority here, with the upper
floors devoted to dining, but when it's brisk out you could do
far worse than pause for a toddy while on a riverside walk.

Golden Eagle

59 Marylebone Lane W1U 2NY
Telephone: 020 7935 3228
Monday-Saturday: 11am-11pm; Sunday: 12noon-10.30pm
Transport: Baker Street, Bond Street

From the street this is a gloomy, even rough-looking place,
thick with green gloss, its doors usually closed. Inside it's quite
different, painted an exuberant shade of lilac, like summer
pudding mixed with cream, with an upright piano that's used
for a sing-along three times a week. Signs urge the customer
to sample the wine list, but the beer shouldn't be overlooked.

The Hand & Shears

1 Middle Street EC1A 7JA
Telephone: 020 7600 0257
Monday–Friday: 11am–11pm
Transport: Barbican

The owners of this wonderful little pub have made the wise
decision to hold on to its three distinct bars – public, saloon and
private, the latter large enough to accommodate a table of three
and perhaps six standing, and there's even a snug too. Despite its
modest size, it has the feeling of a being a place to explore, with
more doors than seems possible for so small a space. A friendly
and attentive landlord with a taste for interesting ales only
adds to its appeal, as does its location off Cloth Fair, a street so
lovely even Sir John Betjeman chose to live here, at number 43.

The Holly Bush

22 Holly Mount NW3 6SG
Telephone: 020 7435 2892
Monday–Saturday: 12noon–11pm; Sunday: 12noon–10.30pm
Transport: Hampstead

Tucked away on a hill in the backstreets of Hampstead, this is
a postcard-perfect setting and a pub to match, with a wooden
interior that has escaped excessive remodelling and 21st-
century tinkering. It's at its best on a golden autumn afternoon,
after a walk on the Heath, with the low sun filtering through
the windows. Food now plays a substantial role in The Holly
Bush's fortunes, but not to the detriment of drinkers.

The Jerusalem Tavern

55 Britton Street EC1M 5UQ
Telephone: 020 7490 4281
Monday-Friday: 11am-11pm
Transport: Farringdon

Bad weather has its benefits, and an excuse to hole up here
for an evening is one of them. Warm and snug, with coal
fires, a front and back room, bar in the middle, creaking
wood floors and the full range of St Peter's ales, there
can be few cosier spots in London. Despite appearances,
it's a relatively new pub, an artful 1990s recreation of
something far older, albeit in a genuine 18th-century
building. It's small, so try to get there early for a seat.

Prince of Wales

53 Highgate High Street N6 5JX
Telephone: 020 8340 0445
Friday & Saturday: 12noon-12midnight;
Sunday-Thursday: 12noon-11pm
Transport: Archway, Highgate

Highgate Village is almost as well-supplied with pubs as
it is estate agents; The Flask gets most attention and others
have done more to modernise themselves, but thankfully
that's not happened here. A small wood-panelled room with
a central bar, it's the sort of place to read a book in peace.
If diversion is required, there are board games, or you might
take a seat by the window and watch the goings-on in the
high street, or perhaps at one of the outside tables by the
rear entrance facing Pond Square. Snug and comfortable,
it would be even better if the service were a little warmer.

The Wrestlers

98 North Road N6 4AA
Telephone: 020 8340 4297
Monday-Thursday: 4.30pm-12midnight; Friday: 4.30pm-1am;
Saturday: 12noon-1am; Sunday: 12noon-11pm
Transport: Archway, Highgate

Frequently very busy, it's worth trying to visit at a quiet time when it smells of leather, wood and, if the huge open fire is lit, of smoke too. Now approaching its 500th anniversary, The Wrestlers was rebuilt in the 1920s, in an unlikely but entirely pleasing mix of contemporary – as in the squared wood panelling – and cod Elizabethan, with stained glass and interior leaded windows behind the bar; only some hideous 1990s wall sconces spoil the effect. Positioned roughly midway between Highgate Wood and Hampstead Heath (directly opposite Berthold Lubetkin's modernist Highpoint flats), it's a popular place for walkers to drop in for a Sunday roast, and it welcomes dogs and families too.

Because half-pints are daintier

The French House

49 Dean Street W1D 5BG
Telephone: 020 7437 2477/2799
Monday–Saturday: 12noon–11pm; Sunday: 12noon–10.30pm
Transport: Leicester Square

There may not be another pub in the land that will reject a customer's simple request for a pint, but here at The French they don't believe in them, nor will they countenance ale. Only lager, cider (French), wines and spirits are available here, yet we love it still. Writing in 1966, Frank Norman said that 'today the drinkers in the French Pub are rather different from those of long ago, but it is still packed with advertising men, actors, a few writers, one or two bums and a great many ordinary people who have popped in for a glass of beer during their lunch hour, and there is never much elbow room.' We are delighted to confirm that all this still holds true today.

For the whole family

Gone are the days of a glass of lemonade outside while the adults enjoyed a pint. All but a few pubs are tolerant of children nowadays: these are some of our favourites.

The Crooked Well

16 Grove Lane SE5 8SY
Telephone: 020 7252 7798
Monday: 5pm-12midnight; Tuesday-Thursday: 12.30pm-12midnight;
Friday & Saturday: 12.30pm-1am; Sunday: 12.30pm-11pm
Transport: Denmark Hill

Just because you have children, that doesn't mean that you have
to become resigned to soft play centres. Equally, it may be the
case that bare lino, a packet of pork scratchings and a dartboard
aren't quite diversion enough for your offspring. Relaxed,
food-oriented pubs are an ideal middle ground, largely free of
potentially hazardous games and with food to keep children
content – at least for a time. This is a particularly good example,
its menu at first glance rather too grown-up and exciting, but
there's a kids one too, so you know you're in the right place.

The Manor Arms

13 Mitcham Lane SW16 6LQ
Telephone: 020 3195 6888
Monday-Wednesday: 12noon-11pm;
Thursday–Saturday: 10am-12midnight;
Sunday: 10am-11pm
Transport: Streatham

If you need nourishment fast for your hungry children, that's no
problem. If you'd prefer that they eat two or three small courses
alongside yours, that's fine too. If you want them to have a
tumbler of Wandle alongside your pint, sorry that's against the
law, but so accommodating and thoughtful is the management
of this pub that your every other requirement will be tended
to. A large garden is handy in the summer, and there are games
and paper to draw on when the weather's bad. All of which
sounds like a recipe for noisy chaos, but somehow it's not.

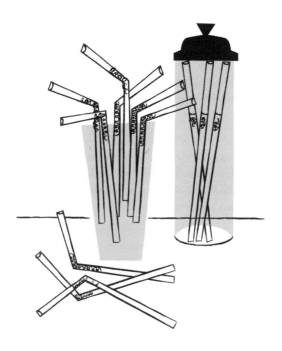

The Marksman

254 Hackney Road E2 7SJ
Telephone: 020 7739 7393
Monday-Saturday: 11am-12midnight; Sunday: 11am-11pm
Transport: Hoxton

Not an obvious place to bring children perhaps, as from
the street it's an inhospitable-looking venue that may
put off passing trade looking for the more picturesque.
Inside there's something of a 1970s Winchester Club
aesthetic, offset by friendly staff and a genuinely convivial
atmosphere with old regulars and new arrivals seemingly at
ease. There's no specific children's menu, and you won't get
any colouring books or Lego bricks, but the fairly-priced
portions of staples are large enough to share, and staff are
accommodating provided you don't expect special treatment.

The Spaniards Inn

Spaniards Road NW3 7JJ
Telephone: 020 8731 8406
Monday-Tuesday: 12noon-11pm; Wednesday-Friday: 12noon to 12midnight;
Saturday: 10am-12midnight; Sunday: 12noon-10.30pm
Transport: Hampstead

A distinctive and historic pub at the edge of Hampstead Heath,
it is a common complaint that The Spaniards is overrun with
children, but in this case we consider that an advantage. Those
in your care will be well catered for with soft drinks and suitable
food, with a large, safe garden to enjoy, while you will be able to
enjoy a restorative drink in preparation for the Heath itself.

When you just want to be alone

Whether through circumstance or choice, spending time on your own in the pub is a thing to savour. There are people to watch, books to read and, for the bold, friends to make.

The Dog & Bell

116 Prince Street SE8 3JD
Telephone: 020 8692 5664
Daily: 12noon–11.30pm
Transport: 47, 188, 199 bus, Deptford

Ale enthusiasts have long worn a path to this backstreet
Deptford pub, which has been winning awards and plaudits
since a time when the words 'real ale drinker' were more
commonly used as an insult than an indicator of discernment.
It remains a beer drinker's delight, with six hand pumps and
a wide range of bottles, but it's also a very homely place that
has a distinctly local feel, with a small garden and that rare
treat, bar billiards.

Fox & Hounds

29 Passmore Street SW1W 8HR
Telephone: 020 7730 6367
Monday–Saturday: 12noon–11pm; Sunday: 12noon–10.30pm
Transport: Sloane Square

Should you find yourself in the chichi backstreets of Chelsea,
this old-fashioned mews-style pub may be just the tonic you
require. Negotiate the abundant hanging baskets and small
front door and you're in a single-room hostelry decorated with
junk-shop finds. From somewhere above comes the sound of
barking dogs, on top of a bookcase stands a stuffed fox, the
barmaid politely but firmly informs a family peering through
the door that their licence forbids children. All is serene.

Ye Grapes

16 Shepherd Market W1J 7QQ
Telephone: 020 7493 4216
Monday–Friday: 11am–11pm; Saturday: 11.30am–11pm;
Sunday: 12noon–10.30pm
Transport: Green Park, Hyde Park

A faintly disreputable atmosphere clings to Shepherd Market,
a warren of streets in the centre of Mayfair where flush-faced
businessmen can be spotted tumbling from anonymous
doorways. For so small an area, it's dense with pubs, this being
the pick of the bunch. Large and haphazard in appearance, it
has plenty of seating, spotted wallpaper perhaps better suited to
a little girl's bedroom and an array of tired Victorian taxidermy
of similar vintage to the building. Food is of the old-fashioned
British type and by now equally old-fashioned Thai variety,
useful ballast for the office workers sharing sweet nothings and
a bottle of white. Amid this atmosphere of indiscretion and
barely contained lust, the solo drinker has so much on which to
speculate that company will be the last thing on your mind.

Red Lion

23 Crown Passage SW1Y 6PP
Telephone: 020 7930 4141
Monday–Saturday: 11am–11pm
Transport: Green Park, St James's Park

An unassuming little place in a tiny passage off Pall Mall,
with a countrified atmosphere that belies its location amid
lofty neighbours including Berry Brothers wine merchants,
James Lock the hatter, most of the surviving gentlemen's clubs
and St James's Palace. Of course one could come here with
friends (many do; it's not unknown for groups to gather on
Monopoly-themed pub crawls) but it's usually so peaceful a
backwater and so modestly proportioned, that visiting with
just a newspaper or book for company seems more suitable.

When you need a place to hide

Bradley's Spanish Bar

42–44 Hanway Street W1T 1UT
Telephone: 020 7636 0359
Monday–Thursday: 12noon–11pm; Friday & Saturday: 12noon–11.30pm;
Sunday: 3pm–10pm
Transport: Tottenham Court Road

It's hardly a secret to anyone reasonably well acquainted with London, but Bradley's manages to retain a sense of the illicit no matter how many familiar faces pass through its doors. A tiny space garlanded with Spanish tchotchkes that reverberates to one of the city's last vinyl jukeboxes stuffed with hits – and some misses – from the 1950s to 1980s, it can get very crowded. On balmy nights, crowds spill on to malodorous Hanway Street, clutching glasses of vino tinto and pints of Cruzcampo. The shy and wary are advised to head to the dimly-lit downstairs.

Lamb & Flag

33 Rose Street WC2E 9EB
Telephone: 020 7497 9504
Monday–Saturday: 11am–11pm; Sun: 12noon–10.30pm
Transport: Covent Garden, Leicester Square

One of London's oldest pubs, it sits at the centre of a small web of alleys, a reminder of the grim rookery Covent Garden once was. Those same streets are what make this a good place to shrug off pursuers, with three different pedestrian routes to take should you see someone you'd rather not – provided, that is, you're among the throng positioned outside. Things are a little less easy inside, where it's long, narrow and frequently crowded. Less good if you're looking to make a quick exit, but with an upstairs room, perhaps not such a bad place to conceal yourself.

Because they like dogs

There seems something profoundly uncivilised about a pub that excludes dogs; restore your faith in human-canine relations at any of the following.

The Albert

11 Princess Road NW1 8JR
Telephone: 020 7722 1886
Monday-Saturday: 11am-11pm; Sunday: 12noon-10.30pm
Transport: Camden Town, Chalk Farm

Of the seven pubs within easy reach of Primrose Hill, this is the last to retain some vestige of an old-fashioned local, albeit with a large open-plan layout and bare board floors that show only faint traces of the separate bars and off-sales area that were once here. Dogs and children are welcome, there's decent food, acceptable ale, friendly staff and, while not outstanding in any way, it's certainly pleasant and reliable, with plenty of space, a conservatory and large garden.

The Colton Arms

187 Greyhound Road W14 9SD
Telephone: 020 7385 6956
Monday-Thursday: 12noon-3pm & 6pm-11.30pm;
Friday: 12noon-3pm & 6pm-12midnight;
Saturday: 12noon-4pm & 7pm-12midnight;
Sunday: 12noon-4pm & 7pm-11pm
Transport: Barons Court, West Kensington

Located in a residential street somewhere between Barons Court and West Kensington, this is an object lesson in how to run a proper pub. The beer is excellent, the landlord amiable, there's a little garden, two small, slightly hidden bars at the back, and the place *gleams*: the copper bar, horse brasses, old till, even the pipes in the gents or, as the sign reads, Sires (there's a Wenches too). Dog owners are welcome to bring their hounds and a gregarious Staffie is resident. With hulking dark oak furniture and a surfeit of timber, the suburban baronial style is not for everyone, but what do they know?

Nelson's Head

32 Horatio Street E2 7EH
Telephone: 020 7729 5595
Monday-Wednesday: 4pm-11pm;
Thursday-Saturday: 3pm-12midnight;
Sunday: 9am-11pm
Transport: Shoreditch High Street

Just off Columbia Road, a winning mix of old-fashioned boozer and high camp, which reaches a crescendo with their annual fancy dress party for dogs, an over-the-top affair that we're surprised hasn't been copied far and wide. Dressing up extends to humans too, and a policy that allows takeaway deliveries means that the choice of food is as varied as the East End can offer.

The Pembury Tavern

90 Amhurst Road E8 1JH
Telephone: 020 8986 8597
Sunday-Thursday: 12noon-11pm;
Friday & Saturday: 12noon-12midnight
Transport: Hackney Central, Hackney Downs

An imposing old pub on a busy intersection, with a very good selection of ale and cider. No original decorative features remain within, leaving it a looking a little bare and cold, but it has many devoted regulars. We applaud the absence of video games and music (seemingly an issue of licensing rather than discretion, but the end result is the same); those looking for diversions may enjoy a game of pool or bar billiards, or a slice of thin-crust pizza cooked in-house. Pets are allowed. Even snakes and ferrets.

The Swan

1 Evershed Walk, 119 Acton Lane W4 5HH
Telephone: 020 8994 8262
Monday-Friday: 5pm-11pm; Saturday: 12noon-11pm;
Sunday: 12noon-10.30pm
Transport: Chiswick Park

Spacious inside, with a pleasant wood-panelled interior and a large garden, throughout all of which dogs (and children) are welcome. Food is now a large part of the operation, with an eye to Europe, but thankfully ales are resolutely British and well kept. Somewhat off the beaten track, it's not the easiest place to find which, given its charms, is perhaps just as well.

Dogs welcome

The Duke of Cambridge

30 St Peter's Street N1 8JT
Telephone: 020 7359 3066
Monday–Saturday: 12noon–11pm;
Sunday: 12noon–10.30pm
Transport: Angel, Essex Road

The Earl Ferrers

22 Ellora Road SW16 6JF
Telephone: 020 8835 8333
Monday & Tuesday: 5pm–11pm;
Wednesday–Friday: 5pm–12midnight;
Saturday: 12noon–12midnight;
Sunday: 12noon–11pm
Transport: Streatham,
Streatham Common

The Elderfield

57 Elderfield Road E5 0LF
Telephone: 020 8986 1591
Monday–Wednesday: 4pm–11pm;
Thursday & Friday: 4pm–12midnight;
Saturday: 1pm–12midnight;
Sunday: 1pm–11pm
Transport: Homerton

The Hare & Billet

1A Hare & Billet Road SE3 0QJ
Telephone: 020 8852 2352
Monday–Wednesday: 12noon–11pm;
Thursday & Friday: 12noon–12midnight;
Saturday: 11am–12midnight;
Sunday: 11am–10.30pm
Transport: Blackheath

The Shaston Arms

4–6 Ganton Street W1F 7QN
Telephone: 020 7287 2631
Monday–Saturday: 12noon–11pm
Transport: Oxford Circus

For the cat

In common with the best bar staff, felines know how to make you feel welcome and relaxed – but mistake them for a pushover and you'll soon suffer the consequences.

The Exmouth Arms

1 Starcross Street NW1 2HR
Telephone: 020 7387 5440
Monday-Thursday: 11am-11pm; Friday: 11am-12midnight;
Saturday: 12noon-11pm
Transport: Euston

There are two things that distinguish this pub located in the
hinterland behind Euston station: an exuberant display of
hanging baskets that does much to enliven a building that's
otherwise quite unremarkable, and Sylvester, a large and
pensive black and white cat who drapes himself wherever he
pleases, with a particular weakness for the bar itself. Another
cat, this one entirely black, answering to the name of Twinkle,
is not the pub's own but can often be seen on the premises,
on occasion catching forty winks in a convenient handbag.

The Harringay Arms

153 Crouch Hill N8 9QH
Telephone: 020 8292 3624
Monday-Thursday: 12noon-1am; Friday-Sunday: 12noon-2am
Transport: 41, 91, W5 bus, Crouch Hill

Try to visit during the day when it's sleepy and friendly, with a
cheery barmaid of many years standing, a handful of regulars,
and an inky black cat stretched languidly across cushioned
seating. Until quite recently an Irish pub, new owners are going
for a younger audience, signalled slightly counter-intuitively
by the array of 1980s record sleeves. Thankfully, the curious
seating arrangement – rows of cushioned benches – and highly
varnished wood panelling have been left untouched.

The Nags Head

9 Orford Road E17 9LP
Telephone: 020 8520 9709
Monday-Saturday: 12noon-11pm; Sunday: 12noon-10.30pm
Transport: Walthamstow Central

Located in the middle of Walthamstow Village, a bucolic patch of E17 that has an attractive church, a large 15th-century half-timbered building and almshouses of only slightly more recent vintage. Cat lovers will appreciate evidence of the esteem in which felines are held here; there's a dedication to the fallen in the garden, and tributes to others in the main room, a light and bright space that – were it not for the bar and pumps – could be a café. Amid cat photos are signs for yoga, pilates and drawing classes in the upstairs Madam La Zongas bar (we're not making this up). A garden with a palm tree is the pub's distinguishing feature.

The Pride of Spitalfields

3 Heneage Street E1 5LJ
Telephone: 020 7247 8933
Monday-Saturday: 11am-11pm; Sunday: 12noon-10.30pm
Transport: Aldgate East, Shoreditch High Street

At the southern end of Brick Lane, just where the curry house barkers are at their most vociferous, is a small turning and, after a few paces, this retreat. As worn and comfortable as an old pair of slippers, the interior is lived-in and unfussy, the ale excellent, and the presence of Lenny, a large and unflappable feline, only adds to its appeal. It's small, with one main bar and a room off to the right, and it can get crowded; not such a bad thing in a place as convivial as this.

The Seven Stars

53-54 Carey Street WC2A 2JB
Telephone: 020 7242 8521
Monday-Friday: 11am-11pm; Saturday: 12noon-11pm;
Sunday: 12noon-10.30pm
Transport: Chancery Lane, Holborn, Temple

An inviting place, comprising three rooms, the two at either
end set up for dining with tables covered in red check
tablecloths. In the middle is the bar, long and shallow with
its ornate mirror advertising 'Foreign wines and spirits'.
Also on the bar are two bowls filled with water and snacks
for Ray Brown, the pub's ruff-wearing cat, a more equable
character than his truculent predecessor, Tom Paine.
'Nothing in common,' explains the barmaid. 'Just cat.'

Tapping The Admiral

77 Castle Road NW1 8SU
Telephone: 020 7267 6118
Monday & Tuesday: 12noon-11pm;
Wednesday-Saturday: 12noon-12midnight;
Sunday: 12noon-10.30pm
Transport: Chalk Farm, Kentish Town West

No two chairs are alike in this lively local, not long ago
brought back from dereliction, but of all the mismatched
pieces, a miniature chaise longue arranged by the fire
stands out in particular. Far too small for a human, it's the
perfect size for Nelson, a black and white cat who rests on
it attracting admiring glances from drinkers. It's easy to see
why Nelson and others like it so much here, with its back
garden, gently lived-in feel and award-winning ale selection.

Because it's beautiful

The voluptuous loveliness of many London pubs is hard
to discern in the after-work throng. Visit these exquisite
examples at mid-afternoon and wallow.

The Blackfriar

174 Queen Victoria Street EC4V 4EG
Telephone: 020 7236 5474
Monday–Thursday: 10am–11.30pm;
Friday & Saturday: 10am–12midnight;
Sunday: 10am–11pm
Transport: Blackfriars

Among the many reasons we have to be grateful to John Betjeman is the survival of this wonderful public house, an opulent art nouveau monument that is merely glorious from the street but quite overwhelming once inside. The interior has a honeyed glow, almost ecclesiastic in atmosphere, with elaborate tile work, copper and plaster friezes, and everywhere disconcertingly jolly monks looming, 'both holy and leering', as one observer noted. It's best visited in the morning or afternoon to avoid the lunch and after-work crowds that can hinder one's appreciation.

Cittie of Yorke

22 High Holborn WC1V 6BN
Telephone: 020 7242 7670
Monday–Saturday: 12noon–11pm
Transport: Chancery Lane, Holborn

Even with the recent vogue for converting banks and cinemas, this is a huge pub. Immensely long and tall, it looks like a medieval banqueting hall with its massive vaulted ceiling, and can be traced to the 15th century, although it was largely rebuilt in the 1920s using original materials. The row of wooden booths is an ideal spot for those with private business to discuss, or trying to keep out of sight; there's also a cellar bar (evenings only) and a cosy front room. For much of the last century it was a branch of Henekeys, which specialised in wine, and their huge vats are still on show around the bar's perimeter. Today it's in the tender embrace of Samuel Smith's, who allow no music or TVs to spoil its very special atmosphere.

Crown & Sugar Loaf

26 Bride Lane EC4Y 8DT
Telephone: 020 7353 3693
Monday–Friday: 12noon–11pm
Transport: City Thameslink

To all appearances, a small but stunning time warp
Victorian pub with mosaic tiled floor, fireplace, marble bar,
etched mirrors all around and leaded windows. Cushioned
benches line the wall facing the bar, and there are tables and
chairs too, with plenty of room for standing. With no TV or
music and an overwhelmingly male clientele, it really does
feel it's from another time, all of which makes its history more
interesting. Originally part of the neighbouring Punch Tavern
on Fleet Street, this only dates from 2004 and its wonderful
interior is new and salvaged.

The Dog and Duck

18 Bateman Street W1D 3AJ
Telephone: 020 7494 0697
Daily: 10am–11pm
Transport: Tottenham Court Road

Less opulent than some others in this section, it has a cosy,
intimate atmosphere conducive to an afternoon drink with a
book – indeed, at any other time it's usually too crowded to be
appreciated. Large, ornate advertising mirrors and wonderful
tilework are notable, as is the treacherous angle of the stairs
down to the loo. One of several pubs claiming a George Orwell
connection, the upstairs dining room is named after him.

The Lamb

94 Lamb's Conduit Street WC1N 3LZ
Telephone: 020 7405 0713
Monday–Wednesday: 12noon–11pm; Thursday–Saturday: 12noon–12midnight;
Sunday: 12noon–10.30pm
Transport: Holborn, Russell Square

Its inviting exterior is clad in two shades of green tile, with gilt ornamental lettering and an attractive hanging lamp, but the greatest allure of The Lamb is inside. Its snob screens, tilting panes of glass that allowed drinkers to order without being seen by the pub's other occupants, are entirely decorative now, but at one time there would have been compartments around the bar (as exist still in the Prince Alfred, page 89). Then there's the Polyphon, a Victorian music machine that can, for a small fee, still be played but usually sits silent. Happily, this is the only music in another wise, calm and conversational pub.

The Palm Tree

127 Grove Road (via Haverfield Road) E3 5BH
Telephone: 020 8980 2918
Monday–Thursday: 12noon–12midnight; Friday & Saturday: 12noon–2am;
Sunday: 12noon–1am (last admission before 11pm)
Transport: Mile End

Beside the canal in what is now Mile End Ecology Park, this two-bar Truman's house is not a classic beauty perhaps, but it's handsome, well-maintained and well-loved too. It has a warm, welcoming glow, in part from the metallic copper wallpaper within. On its walls are photographs of the changing area, minor celebrities and what's rumoured to be Frank Sinatra in the company of the daughter of the house. On weekends a house band sets up in the front bar, with a rotating group of guest singers, resplendently-dressed for the occasion. The back bar is quieter, but notable for the display of caricatures of boxers. It's easy to feel that pubs like this were once the norm, but we suspect it was always in a class of its own.

The Prince Alfred

5A Formosa Street W9 1EE
Telephone: 020 7286 3287
Monday–Thursday: 12noon–11pm;
Friday & Saturday: 12noon–12midnight;
Sunday: 12noon–10.30pm
Transport: Warwick Avenue

Amid the iced-cake streets of Maida Vale stands this elegant pub, stately and graceful with light ironwork and large curved windows. It's less heavy than many Victorian pubs, with an elegant, even airy, atmosphere. There are five bars arranged around a central serving area, each with its own street entrance. Separated from one another by screens of carved wood and etched glass, intact 19th-century snob screens allow drinkers to avoid the sight or gaze of others. A connected dining room is entirely modern in appearance.

Princess Louise

208 High Holborn WC1V 7EP
Telephone: 020 7405 8816
Monday–Friday: 11.30am–11pm; Saturday: 12noon–11pm;
Sunday: 12noon–10.30pm
Transport: Holborn

A few years ago the Princess Louise was refurbished by its owner Samuel Smith's, the magnificent tile work, plaster ceilings, mirrors and carved wood restored and its 1870s floorplan reinstated, with a series of drinking compartments for small groups to gather in peaceful seclusion arranged around a deep central bar. Only the requirement that gentlemen wear whiskers and top hats could improve it. Even the gents is spectacular (and Grade II listed), with its massive marble urinals and tiled floor.

The Red Lion

2 Duke of York Street SW1Y 6JP
Telephone: 020 7321 0782
Monday–Saturday: 11.30am–11pm
Transport: Piccadilly Circus

On a good day the sun's rays filter through the windows catching the array of polished mirrors, bevelled glass and rich wood that decorates this diminutive but immaculate Victorian specimen, which was rebuilt in the 1870s with little changed since, bar a bit of sprucing up in the early 1960s. Such is its size there's not much in the way of comfortable seating, but it's not somewhere you should plan to linger. Instead, stop in for a refresher, savour the surroundings and march on.

The Salisbury

90 St Martin's Lane WC2N 4AP
Telephone: 020 7836 5863
Monday–Thursday: 11.30am–11pm; Friday & Saturday: 11am–12am;
Sunday: 12noon–10.30pm
Transport: Covent Garden, Leicester Square

A pub that's as opulent and showy as the theatres that surround it, with carved mahogany bar and pillars, candelabras, decorative mirrors, engraved glass and deep, padded seating in semi-circular arrangements. A small area at one side of the bar has its own entrance from St Martin's Court and is shielded from public view. There are a few modern distractions, chiefly the signs extolling their menu, and a room at the back is relatively new, but this is a magnificent establishment, with the added benefit of pleasant bar staff.

PRIVATE BAR

The Tabard

2 Bath Road W4 1LW
Telephone: 020 8994 3492
Sunday–Wednesday: 12noon–11pm;
Thursday–Saturday: 12noon–12midnight
Transport: Turnham Green

In Bedford Park, a late Victorian Arts and Crafts suburb that's all red brick and organic shapes, with a lovely common and human-scale housing; this pub may just be its jewel. It's hard to choose between public and saloon bars; the former has wonderful decorative tiles, carved-wood panelling and brass door furniture, over on the other side it's cushioned and comfortable, more dimly lit with a small sunken recess at the back, panelled in wood with high-backed, soft leather upholstery. In addition to all this, the welcome is warm and the ale selection very good.

The Viaduct Tavern

126 Newgate Street EC1A 7AA
Telephone: 020 7600 1863
Monday–Friday: 8.30am–11pm
Transport: City Thameslink, St Paul's

Should you find yourself staggering from the Old Bailey in need of a stiff drink, fortification is available directly opposite in this stately semi-circular Victorian pub, constructed at the eastern end of Holborn Viaduct. Those in a more contemplative mood may pause to take in the etched glass, gilded mirrors, three paintings of sorrowful maidens and abundant carved woodwork. The pub's original separate drinking areas are long gone, but one rare surviving feature is an elegant booth of etched glass and carved wood at the back of the bar that would have been used as an office of sorts by the landlord.

The Victoria

10A Strathearn Place W2 2NH
Telephone: 020 7724 1191
Monday–Saturday: 11am–11pm; Sunday: 12noon–10.30pm
Transport: Lancaster Gate, Paddington

Writing in 1966, architecture critic Ian Nairn described this as 'one of the best London pub rooms, dark and plushy and glowing', and so it remains today, as ornate, gleaming and comfortable as it must have been 150 years ago. Five globe lights rise from the mahogany bar on brass posts, reflected in extravagantly decorated mirrors, woodwork is carved, original pictures abound. Even the digital till and rubberised mats of the present day barely spoil the atmosphere. Upstairs are rooms for hire, the small Library Bar and larger Theatre Bar constructed in the 1950s using fittings from a Victorian theatre.

The Warrington Hotel

93 Warrington Crescent W9 1EH
Telephone: 020 7286 8282
Monday–Thursday: 11am–11pm;
Friday & Saturday: 11am–12 midnight;
Sunday: 12noon–10.30pm
Transport: Warwick Avenue

Sullied somewhat by a brief and inglorious period as part of Gordon Ramsay's portfolio, this grand old Edwardian hotel-turned-pub appears to be back on form. It's huge, sitting proudly on a peaceful roundabout, with tiled columns and doorway. Inside it's divided into two large rooms with art nouveau stained glass, marble columns and acres of space. It's no surprise that it feels more like a hotel lobby than a pub, although the left-hand bar is perhaps a tad more intimate.

The Newton Arms

33 Newton Street WC2B 5EL
Telephone: 020 7242 8797
Monday-Saturday: 11am-11pm
Transport: Holborn

It can be hard to identify what future generations will treasure
– after all, it's not so long ago that Victorian features were
considered ugly and fussy. These days, the box-shaped pubs of
the 1960s to 1980s are largely reviled for their lack of character,
but that may change with the passing of time. For now, The
Newton Arms is an archetype of the style; brightly lit, with
Sky Sports, a garish carpet and barmen in white short-sleeved
shirts and black ties. Off the beaten track, on the edge of
Covent Garden, for now it's just waiting to be rediscovered.

The Shakespeares Head

1 Arlington Way EC1R 1XA
Telephone: 020 7837 2581
Daily: 11.30am-11.30pm
Transport: Angel

Its hard edges softened by hanging baskets, the low-slung,
brick-built Shakespeare is gloriously untouched by the fads
that have ruined the character of nearby Upper Street. Situated
just behind Sadler's Wells, it has two quite different purposes,
as overflow for audience and performers and as a cheerful local.
The result is that photographs of pub beanos vie for wall space
with signed posters for revered dance troupes, the lavatory
signs feature pirouetting dancers, and a bell rings to signal
performances. That's a strange mix, one which is overseen ably
by charming bar staff who serve drinks as unreconstructed as
the 1970s interior.

When conversation isn't enough

Topics of the day and tittle-tattle can only go so far. There are times when we require entertainment, not from friends but from professionals. Or at least enthusiastic amateurs.

The Dublin Castle

94 Parkway NW1 7AN
Telephone: 020 7485 1773
Monday–Wednesday: 1pm–1am; Thursday: 1pm–2am;
Friday–Sunday: 12noon–2am
Transport: Camden Town

A live music venue since the 1970s, what's more impressive than the names of those who played here and went on to make it (a list that's hardly insubstantial), is that hopeful acts continue to perform most nights of the week in surroundings that have been little altered in thirty years. Still a family pub, it's never been colonised by a particular subculture, its own personality being stronger than those who've visited. The large bar area with glittering tabletops and peculiar fake half-timbering is entirely separate from the live room and still free to get in, even late at night.

Joe's

78-79 Chalk Farm Road NW1 8AR
Telephone: 020 7018 2168
Daily: 5pm–3am
Transport: Chalk Farm

There is much to be said for keeping it simple, which is precisely what has been done here. Directly opposite the Roundhouse, it's open late, DJs play 1950s and 1960s rock 'n' roll and R&B every night, there are hot dogs for the hungry and drinks for the thirsty. There's even proper ale, just one pump, but as this is part of the Southampton Arms stable, you can be confident it's good. Depending on how early you arrive you may wonder how they stay in business, by midnight you'll ask why there aren't more places like it.

The Lexington

96-98 Pentonville Road N1 9JB
Telephone: 020 7837 5371
Sunday-Wednesday: 12noon-2am; Thursday: 12noon-3am;
Friday & Saturday: 12noon-4am
Transport: King's Cross

Starting life as The Belvedere Tavern, there have been licensed premises here since 1780, but after 200 years it had lost its way. New management arrived in 2008, renaming it The Lexington and with that, order has been restored and its future seems safe. At ground level is a bar with a special dedication to American whiskey and several US and British beers. Swagged red velvet curtains set the tone and help to damp the echo of the large room, you can see traces of a 1970s refit in the raised seating area with fake fire, but the atmosphere is closer to bar than pub, more so as the day moves on with a loud jukebox and DJs. A large upstairs venue has 200-person capacity and is used for live shows, literary events, Rough Trade's pop quiz and jumble sales.

The Montpelier

43 Choumert Road SE15 4AR
Telephone: 020 7635 9483
Sunday-Wednesday: 12noon-11pm; Thursday: 12noon-12midnight;
Friday & Saturday: 12noon-1am
Transport: Peckham Rye

There are so many reasons for couples to argue, let us be grateful that The Montpelier has resolved at least one: going to the pub or pictures is no longer a debate. Their back room doubles as a cinema, which means everyone can be happy. Blockbusters are off the menu, this is a place to see new independent releases and classics of a slightly arty bent for the bargain price of £3. They also host exhibitions and DJs on Saturday nights. Food and drink are good too in this hardworking, cheerful pub that's been modernised and given a touch of the junk shop aesthetic, but with a light touch that others could learn from.

Ye Olde Rose & Crown

53 Hoe Street E17 4SA
Telephone: 020 8509 3880
Monday-Thursday: 10am-11pm;
Friday & Saturday: 10am-12midnight;
Sunday: 12noon-11pm
Transport: Walthamstow Central

Bearing the scars of numerous refits and changes of direction, this is not the prettiest place – although there are some hints of former grandeur in the mosaic tiles by the gents. At times the atmosphere is closer to a community centre with a notable selection of ale than a pub, which is perhaps not surprising given the variety of events that are hosted in the main bar and two additional rooms. A frenetic booking policy means that on any given day something is sure to be on, ranging from a DJ playing 78s from the 1920s to 1950s to a folk club, quizzes, comedy or theatre.

Sebright Arms

31-35 Coate Street E2 9AG
Telephone: 020 7729 0937
Monday-Wednesday: 5pm-11pm;
Thursday-Saturday: 5pm-12midnight;
Sunday: 12noon-10.30pm
Transport: Cambridge Heath

A redoubtable little pub that has been a music hall (a real one and a 1980s approximation), disco, heavy metal club and in 2009, almost became a block of flats. After a narrow escape from the developers, it's now a thriving live music venue and host to Lucky Chip burgers, in what may be the world's longest pop-up. The choice of ale is as unerring as the booking policy, guaranteeing a tight squeeze most nights of the week. Their sister operation, The Miller, is listed on page 107.

THE ROSE & CROWN

The Snooty Fox

75 Grosvenor Avenue N5 2NN
Telephone: 020 7354 9532
Monday–Thursday: 4pm–11pm; Friday: 4pm–1am;
Saturday: 12noon–1am;
Sunday: 12noon–10.30pm
Transport: Canonbury

A popular local with plenty going for it: outdoor seating, decent food, a good and changing range of ale and friendly staff. There are DJs on Fridays and Saturdays, and on other nights a jukebox that might benefit from a slightly firmer grasp on the volume control – conversation isn't always easy. The walls are dotted with pictures of familiar musical heroes and villains (Shane MacGowan, Serge Gainsbourg, Johnny Cash et al), a decorative style these days perhaps more redolent of student bedrooms than nonconformist joie de vivre.

Further distraction

Amersham Arms

388 New Cross Road SE14 6TY
Telephone: 020 8469 1499
Sunday–Wednesday: 12noon–12midnight;
Thursday–Saturday: 12noon–3am
Transport: New Cross,
New Cross Gate

The Brown Derby

336 Kennington Park Road SE11 4PP
Telephone: 020 7735 5122
Monday: 4pm–11pm;
Tuesday–Sunday: 12noon–1am
Transport: Oval

The Griffin

93 Leonard Street EC2A 4RD
Telephone: 020 7739 6719
Monday–Friday: 11am–12midnight;
Saturday: 11am–1am;
Sunday: 12noon–12midnight
Transport: Old Street

The Half Moon

93 Lower Richmond Road SW15 1EU
Telephone: 020 8780 9383
Sunday–Thursday: 11am–11pm;
Friday & Saturday: 11am–1am
Transport: Putney

The Half Moon

10 Half Moon Lane SE24 9HU
Telephone: 020 7274 2733
Monday–Thursday: 11am–1am;
Friday & Saturday: 11am–2am;
Sunday: 12noon–10.30pm
Transport: Herne Hill

The Miller

96 Snowsfields Road SE1 3SS
Telephone: 020 7407 2690
Monday–Wednesday: 12noon–11pm;
Thursday: 12noon–12midnight;
Friday: 12noon–1am;
Saturday: 6pm–1am
Transport: Borough, London Bridge

The Shacklewell Arms

71 Shacklewell Lane E8 2EB
Telephone: 020 7249 0810
Monday–Wednesday: 5pm–12midnight;
Thursday: 5pm–1am; Friday: 5pm–3am;
Saturday: 12noon–3am;
Sunday: 12noon–12midnight
Transport: Dalston Kingsland

The Windmill

22 Blenheim Gardens SW2 5BZ
Telephone: 020 8671 0700
Opening times vary, so check the pub
website for the latest details.
Transport: Brixton

When you have people to see

Whether you need space for a large group, or diversions to fill awkward silences, we're here to help.

The Bricklayer's Arms

32 Waterman Street SW15 1DD
Telephone: 020 8789 0222
Daily: 12noon–11pm
Transport: Putney, Putney Bridge

When topics of the day have grown tired and gossip is exhausted, there is no better way to pass the time with friends than an absorbing round of skittles or shove ha'penny, both of which remain popular at this unpretentious tavern. Although both games reward skill and practice, neither is a requisite and a good time can be had by a novice without fear of humiliation or injury. Also worth noting is The Bricklayer's formidable range of real ale and cider – equally well suited to celebrating victories and softening defeat.

The Clapton Hart

231 Lower Clapton Road E5 8EG
Telephone: 020 8985 8124
Monday–Wednesday: 4pm–11pm;
Thursday & Friday: 4pm–12midnight;
Saturday: 12noon–12midnight;
Sunday: 12noon–11pm
Transport: Clapton

After an unhappy incarnation as Chimes, the former White Hart has been brought back to life with a keen eye to the desires of the current, and future, inhabitants of Clapton: that means a large, careful beer selection, hearty seasonal food and a tolerant attitude to children. The decorative approach might be described as advanced desiccation, with exposed brick, bare plaster, taxidermy, old signs and antique table football, but the seating, though seemingly arbitrary in style and pattern, is suspiciously comfortable and well upholstered. Beneath its careworn appearance, this is a sharp operation at work. The pub's enormous size makes it suitable for meetings and assignations of all types, from sit-down meals to class reunions.

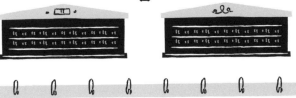

Express Tavern

Kew Bridge Road TW8 0EW
Telephone: 020 8560 8484
Monday–Thursday: 11.30am–3pm & 5.30pm–11pm;
Friday: 11.30am–3pm & 5.30pm–12midnight;
Saturday: 11.30am–3pm & 6.30pm–12midnight;
Sunday: 12noon–11pm
Transport: Kew Bridge

You'll have no need for conversational cue cards here, it's the sort of place where the well-embedded locals ensure that there's always something to focus attention on. Failing that, there are enough decorative curiosities to hold one's interest for at least a couple of drinks, and a large garden too. Admittedly, it's not a central location, but it's family-run with good ale and convenient for a Thames stroll.

Glasshouse Stores

55 Brewer Street W1F 9UL
Telephone: 020 7287 5278
Monday–Saturday: 12noon–11pm; Sunday: 12noon–10.30pm
Transport: Piccadilly Circus

Even as offices empty and the streets are thronged, there's usually room to sit and chat in peace at this deceptively spacious Samuel Smith's pub. Windows front and back catch the last of the sun's rays, and a large downstairs bar is available when things get busy – in theory at least, its stated 6pm opening time is not strictly adhered to. Sadly the bar billiards table seems to have fallen into disrepair, but there's always darts if the lust for competition arises.

Prince of Wales

48 Cleaver Square SE11 4EA
Telephone: 020 7735 9916
Monday–Saturday: 12noon–11pm; Sunday: 12noon–10.30pm
Transport: Kennington

In a tall and handsome red-brick building at the north-west edge of an attractive Georgian residential square that appears unscathed by either bombs or developers, is this nice little local that few outsiders would visit were it not for its proximity to the Oval cricket ground. There's another reason too: in summer the square is used for games of pétanque (a variant of boules so slight you may not notice), which has the double benefit of providing activity to fill the gaps in flagging chat or, at the very least, a conversation-starter.

Because you need to meet first

Or perhaps somewhere to convene after. Either way, what follows is a selection that's ideally suited for places of cultural interest – and a couple of railway terminals too.

Cultural centres

BARBICAN
The Two Brewers

121 Whitecross Street EC1Y 8JH
Monday-Saturday: 11am-11pm; Sunday: 12noon-11pm
Transport: Barbican

Conveniently located for the Barbican Centre, it's also
right by Whitecross Street's eponymous market and
street food vendors. All the better, then, that the Brewers
has no kitchen but allows customers to bring their own
food, as long as they buy a drink. It's a cheery place, with
an interesting mix of customers drawn from the various
cultural events taking place nearby as well as local estates.

EARLS COURT
The Atlas

16 Seagrave Road SW6 1RX
Telephone: 020 7385 9129
Monday-Saturday: 12noon-11pm; Sunday: 12noon-10.30pm
Transport: West Brompton

Should it be your misfortune to attend an event at Earls
Court, let this be your consolation. Food, wine and what they
call 'fizz' get the big push, but there's decent ale too. Best of
all is the room itself, evidently extensively renovated by
Truman in the 1930s, with two brick fireplaces displaying
the brewery's iconography, serving hatches, and the names
of extinct and neglected drinks neatly lettered around the
perimeter on the panelled walls: Burton Bitter, Barley Wine,
London Stout. There's a large upstairs room for hire and
if the interior palls, a garden too.

O2 Centre
The Pelton Arms

23-25 Pelton Road SE10 9PQ
Telephone: 020 8858 0572
Monday-Thursday: 12noon-12midnight;
Friday & Saturday: 12noon-1am;
Sunday: 12noon-11pm
Transport: Maze Hill

There can be nowhere that's truly convenient for the O2, but this has the looked-for combination of being geographically close (about 15 minutes by bus) and worlds apart in every other way. Large and ramshackle, with a good selection of ale and filled with detritus of a type that nearby Greenwich Market once specialised in: stuffed animals, a wind-up gramophone, a collection of soda syphons. There's also a garden, dart board and bar billiards too, and with so much entertainment it's good to know that families are welcome. It's worth noting that there's live music on Friday and Saturday nights, which may spoil any attempt to relax before visiting the O2.

Museums at South Kensington
The Hour Glass

279-283 Brompton Road SW3 2DY
Telephone: 020 7581 2840
Monday-Thursday: 12noon-11pm;
Friday & Saturday: 12noon-11.30pm;
Sunday: 12noon-10.30pm
Transport: South Kensington

Long and shallow, with just a few tables and stools to perch on, this is near enough the South Kensington museums that it makes for a good place to restore yourself before or after, but not so close that it's packed with other visitors. Five benches outside are a pleasant good weather option.

TATE MODERN
The Cockpit

7 St Andrew's Hill EC4V 5BY
Telephone: 020 7248 7315
Monday-Saturday: 11am-11pm; Sunday: 12noon-10.30pm
Transport: Blackfriars, City Thameslink, St Paul's

The last cockfight held here was more than 150 years ago, these days it's a friendly gathering space, with regulars lined up at the bar cheerily making fun of each other and framed pictures of strutting roosters on the walls. Look up and you can see the gallery from which spectators viewed fights – although there are some doubts as to its authenticity. On a tight corner with Ireland Yard, where Shakespeare undoubtedly lived, the pub is V-shaped and painted black with details and lettering picked out jauntily in gold and red. Although on the other side of the river to Tate Modern, it's just a short walk, and a rather spectacular one at that.

BRICK LANE
The Carpenter's Arms

73 Cheshire Street E2 6EG
Telephone: 020 7739 6342
Monday-Wednesday: 4pm-11.30pm;
Thursday & Sunday: 12noon-11.30pm;
Friday & Saturday: 12noon-12.30am
Transport: Bethnal Green, Shoreditch High Street

Small, sensitively renovated pub that neatly combines East End old and new. Good ales and food, and a location that's just far enough off the beaten track for everyone's comfort. The small beer garden is a rare treat for the area, and an added incentive to visit, if such a thing were needed.

BRITISH MUSEUM
The Museum Tavern

49 Great Russell Street WC1B 3BA
Telephone: 020 7242 8987
Monday-Thursday: 11am-11.30pm;
Friday & Saturday: 11am-12midnight;
Sunday: 10am-10pm
Transport: Tottenham Court Road, Holborn

It's not letting you in on a secret to say that this is the most convenient pub in which to restore yourself after the British Museum – it's directly opposite, after all. What's surprising is that it's usually not too crowded, more popular with local office workers than tourists. The interior is quite handsome, most notably the attractive carved bar.

O2 ACADEMY, BRIXTON
The Duke of Edinburgh

204 Ferndale Road SW9 8AG
Telephone: 020 7326 0301
Monday-Thursday: 3pm-12midnight; Friday: 2pm–2am;
Saturday: 12noon-2am; Sunday: 12noon–11pm
Transport: Brixton, Clapham North

Substantial on the outside, within it's decorated in a style that might kindly be characterised as junk-shop eclectic – mismatched furniture and lights, wall-mounted animal heads – which detracts a little from some quite nice original features. In summer the very large garden has a transformative effect and is the pub's main draw. Even in winter, it's comfortable, drinks are good and so is the food, none of which can be said of the Academy, which is a 10-minute walk away.

TATE BRITAIN
Morpeth Arms

58 Millbank SW1P 4RW
Telephone: 020 7834 6442
Monday-Friday: 11am-11pm; Saturday: 11am-11.30pm;
Sunday: 12noon-11pm
Transport: Pimlico

Young's pubs were until recently respectable, serviceable places, each displaying a photograph of the Queen Mother pulling a pint and serving tasty if unadventurous beer – it's no accident that their bitter is also known as Ordinary. Their current approach is to aggressively promote very average food, use blackboards for comic effect and plaster their buildings in loud wallpaper. The Morpeth Arms is no exception, but its location on this gloomy stretch of riverside makes it handy for the Tate and the upstairs Spying Room just about gives views across the Thames, although with construction directly ahead, that may not be the case much longer.

BUFFALO BAR / THE GARAGE / UNION CHAPEL
The Compton Arms

4 Compton Avenue N1 2XD
Telephone: 020 7359 6883
Sunday-Thursday: 12noon-11pm;
Friday & Saturday: 12noon-12midnight
Transport: Highbury & Islington

A couple of roads back from Upper Street and a world away in atmosphere, in a quiet road that feels (at least at its southern end) like a country lane, this little pub is just what you'd expect to see in such a place. Plain, unflashy and unadorned, its only ornament is dimpled crown glass windows either side of the door. If it weren't for the three televisions, one of which is in the small back garden, even former habitué and near neighbour George Orwell might approve.

PALE AND STOCK ALES

GUARANTEED MALT AND HOPS

Stations

KING'S CROSS / ST PANCRAS
The Queen's Head

66 Acton Street WC1X 9NB
Telephone: 0207 713 5772
Tuesday–Saturday: 12noon–12midnight;
Sunday & Monday: 12noon–11pm

If you have time to spare between trains at King's Cross
or St Pancras and are not overly burdened by luggage, we
estimate that it is no more than a ten-minute walk here from
any platform, despite its somewhat out-of-the-way location.
Occupying a single terraced building with some nice original
fixtures and even an upright piano, it's surprisingly large inside
with plenty of room to stretch after an irksome journey, and
two skylights bringing in natural light. An excellent range of
ale and the usual cheese and meat platters and other hearty
fare should be just what you need before or after your travels.

VICTORIA
The Cask & Glass

39–41 Palace Street SW1E 5HN
Telephone: 020 7834 7630
Monday–Friday: 11am–11pm; Saturday: 12noon–8pm

There are just five tables in this little inn that goes quietly
about its business in the shadow of the new Cardinal
Place shopping mall, just minutes from Victoria station.
Pretty hanging baskets adorn the front and the interior
retains its ornamental Shepherd Neame branding over
and behind the bar. It is a modest, friendly place and
a refuge in one of the city's less-hospitable areas.

If you must go to a gastropub

The Eagle

159 Farringdon Road EC1R 3AL
Telephone: 020 7837 1353
Monday–Saturday: 12noon–11pm; Sunday: 12noon–5pm
Transport: Farringdon

For a sense of what the phrase gastropub means in its original coinage, pay a visit to what in all likelihood was the first and is still among the best of the breed. It remains much as it did when it opened in 1991, a pared-back room with an open kitchen, drinkers and eaters mingling happily. Orders are taken at the bar, there are no tablecloths, no waiters and prices remain most reasonable. The chalkboard menu changes regularly, but a steak sandwich is usually available and always terrific.

Because a story goes with it

Dark histories, eccentric landlords, architectural oddities: these are pubs with a past.

The Barley Mow

8 Dorset Street W1U 6QW
Telephone: 020 7487 4773
Monday–Saturday: 12noon–11pm
Transport: Baker Street

Just because you look for beautiful and historic pubs, it's no guarantee your friends will be as enthusiastic. Here, then, is somewhere for the unreconstructed drinker as much as the keen-eyed student of vernacular architecture. A plain but handsome exterior with three separate entrances, inside it's notable for a cheerful scruffiness and a pair of three-walled boxes attached to the left side of the bar that are big enough to hide a few drinkers from general view, but give free access to mine host. There are various theories as to their original use, none definitive, but the cubbyholes are not elaborate in any way, they look more like something knocked up by a skilled amateur than a master craftsman.

The George Inn

75–77 Borough High Street SE1 1NH
Telephone: 020 7407 2056
Monday–Saturday: 11am–11pm; Sunday: 12noon–10.30pm
Transport: London Bridge

Whether it's the bloodless grip of its owner The National Trust or uninspired management by tenant Greene King, or perhaps just the weight of history and expectation, the city's only surviving galleried coaching inn is not so much an enjoyable a place to have a drink as it is an interesting place to visit. The first room, The Parliament Bar, is perhaps most atmospheric, although a chalkboard advertising 'Three for two on wines' breaks the spell. For all that, there's nothing like it.

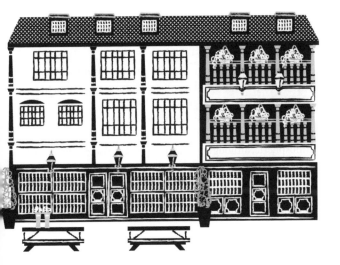

The Golden Heart

110 Commercial Street E1 6LZ
Telephone: 020 7247 2158
Monday-Saturday: 11am-11pm; Sunday: 12noon-10.30pm
Transport: Liverpool Street, Shoreditch High Street

The story here is that of Sandra Esquilant, perhaps the country's most famous publican, adored by Tracey Emin, Gilbert and George, Jake and Dinos Chapman, as well as dozens of others who have found refuge in this substantial pub opposite Spitalfields Market, its traditional exterior now adorned with neon by Emin. Not all have taken equally to Sandra, nor she to them, but be polite and buy a proper drink and you shouldn't have too much trouble.

The Grenadier

18 Wilton Row SW1X 7NR
Telephone: 020 7235 3074
Daily: 12noon-11pm
Transport: Hyde Park Corner, Knightsbridge

Famed as London's most haunted licensed premises, and situated in a movie-set-pretty mews with a bright red sentry box outside, The Grenadier is in danger of being no more than a tourist attraction. Visit at the right time though, say three o'clock on a Wednesday afternoon, and you can see why it's appeared in every London guidebook of the last 50 years. There are two small bars off the main room – The Wellington Room and The Boot Room – all three are small and dark, with militaria on the walls and bank notes of various currencies attached to the ceiling. The pewter bar is a rare survivor.

King & Queen

1 Foley Street W1W 6DL
Telephone: 020 7636 5619
Monday-Saturday: 11am-11pm; Sunday: 7pm-10.30pm
Transport: Goodge Street

Nothing in the world of Bob Dylan is entirely straightforward, nevertheless the common consensus is that he made his UK debut here in the winter of 1962, after being spotted in the audience by Martin Carthy at the upstairs folk club. More than 50 years on, a folk club still gathers here every Friday, with a small but devoted following. Though rather hidden, it's a beautiful pub and we challenge anyone to walk past the florid gilded K and Q on the double doors and not want to push through.

The Old Bell Tavern

95 Fleet Street EC4Y 1DH
Telephone: 020 7583 0216
Monday-Friday: 11am-11pm; Saturday: 12noon-8pm;
Sunday: 12noon-5pm
Transport: City Thameslink

Best approached via the passage to the side of St Bride's Church, which is directly behind, and for the renovation of which after the Great Fire, Sir Christopher Wren had this pub built on a site that had previously been occupied by several other hostelries. It has undergone extensive refurbishment over the years and Wren's builders have been replaced by printers, journalists and latterly office workers, but it's a pleasant place, particularly when it's warm enough to take drinks outside, facing the tranquil churchyard.

Ye Olde Cheshire Cheese

REBUILT 1667

Ye Olde Cheshire Cheese

145 Fleet Street EC4A 2BU
Telephone: 020 7353 6170
Monday-Saturday: 11.30am-11.30pm
Transport: Blackfriars, City Thameslink, Temple

We won't speculate at what point tourists began to outnumber regulars, but probably long after Thackeray, Dickens, Boswell and Johnson had supped from their last flagon, not that it's changed much in the intervening years. There are rooms of varying sizes, some just for dining, others for drinking, reached via narrow corridors and creaking staircases. A 'ye olde' prefix can rankle, but this is a genuinely historic site – a hostelry has stood here since the 16th century.

The Star Tavern

6 Belgrave Mews West SW1X 8HT
Telephone: 020 7235 3019
Monday-Friday: 11am-11pm; Saturday: 12noon-11pm;
Sunday: 12noon-10.30pm
Transport: Knightsbridge

A well looked-after little pub set amid embassies and the homes of the super-rich. It's comfortable enough, with a small bar, a restaurant-style area, two fires and large rugs, but its mainly known for its 1960s heyday, when it was a meeting place for high society, movie stars and the demi-monde, presided over by a fabulously rude landlord. The Great Train Robbery was allegedly planned here, a claim also made for The Spencer Arms in Putney and the lamented Ship & Blue Ball in Shoreditch.

For that Patrick Hamilton feeling

The Duke

7 Roger Street WC1N 2PB
Telephone: 020 7242 7230
Monday-Saturday: 12noon-11pm; Sunday: 12noon-10pm
Transport: Holborn, Russell Square

There is an authentically melancholy between-the-wars atmosphere here, lent in part by the 1930s fittings and also the staff, whose demeanour is, as PG Wodehouse might say, far from being gruntled. The rear half of The Duke is a restaurant, but we favour the front, particularly on a drizzly afternoon, with only a battered Penguin paperback and a half of something flat and bitter for company.

Horse and Groom

128 Great Portland Street W1W 6PS
Telephone: 020 7580 4726
Monday-Saturday: 11am-11pm; Sunday: 12noon-10.30pm
Transport: Great Portland Street

Contemplation is easy in the Horse & Groom's sepia light, with chequered floor and ceramic tiles, one's thoughts only interrupted by the occasional thud of dart landing on board or the rustle of a newspaper. This Samuel Smith's pub has less of the after-work crush than neighbouring establishments, but is still best enjoyed on a quiet afternoon.

Because the beer's so good

Of course pubs are about much more than just drinking, but the art of brewing, keeping and serving fine ales shouldn't be overlooked.

The Bree Louise

69 Cobourg Street NW1 2HH
Telephone: 020 7681 4930
Monday-Saturday: 11.30am-12midnight; Sunday: 12noon-10.30pm
Transport: Euston

Brightly-lit, with low ceilings and municipal in atmosphere, it's testament to The Bree Louise's enormous and excellent range of beer and cider that it's usually hard to find a seat here, and the outside is often busy too even in colder weather. Home-made pies come recommended, with the unfortunate consequence that the smell of cooking seems permanently trapped within.

The Camden Town Brewery

55 Wilkin Street Mews NW5 3NN
Telephone: 020 7485 1671
Thursday-Saturday: 12noon-11pm
Transport: Kentish Town, Kentish Town West

In a railway arch next to their own brewery in the industrial backstreets of Kentish Town, it may not look much like a pub – blond wood, white tiles, not a horsebrass in sight – and its opening hours are limited, but as a community hub, they do a pretty good job. Making use of a large outside area, each Saturday in summer a different food stand sets up to cook and sell, and there's often a DJ too. It can get busy, so off sales are a good option and for locals, refillable growlers may prove addictive.

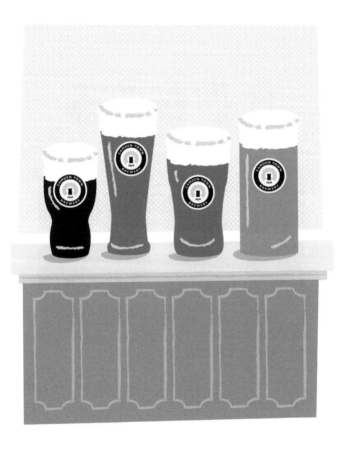

The Cock Tavern

315 Mare Street E8 1EJ
Monday-Thursday: 12noon-11pm; Friday: 12noon-1am;
Saturday: 12noon-12midnight; Sunday: 12noon-10.30pm
Transport: Hackney Central

An appearance of effortlessness is the mark of greatness – it's true across the board: dancers, magicians, writers, artists and publicans too. As with its sister The Southampton Arms (see page 184), The Cock Tavern is about keeping it simple and doing it well. A pub of medium size with dark wood walls, plain stools and wooden settles, there's a jukebox that's not too loud, lighting that's low enough to flatter but not so dim that you'll squint, there are scotch eggs and pork pies to eat, and a range of up to 16 cask ales, including their own Howling Hops. And just so you know they have a sense of humour, there's a patch of cement out back they call a garden.

The Craft Beer Co.

82 Leather Lane EC1N 7TR
Monday-Saturday: 12noon-11pm; Sunday: 12noon-10.30pm
Transport: Farringdon

There are more than 30 beers on draught alone and three large fridges packed full of bottles from small breweries around the world, so clearly this is a pub aimed at ale nerds, but such connoisseurship is not obligatory and staff are glad to help with choices. Formerly The Clockhouse, a rough and ready market pub, some effort has been made to retain original features, most notably the mirrored ceiling marked with the hours of the day, a large Courage brewery mirror and there's a clock high up on the exterior too. Its atmosphere is certainly modern though, with wallpaper emblazoned with the company logo and high, rather comfortable seating that feels a long way from the dark, slouchy pubs of old. They also have branches in Brixton, Clapham, Islington and Brighton.

The Dean Swift

10 Gainsford Street SE1 2NE
Telephone: 020 7357 0748
Sunday–Thursday: 12noon–12midnight;
Friday & Saturday: 12noon–1am
Transport: Bermondsey, London Bridge

A crisp, white room that feels more like a restaurant than a pub, but has a notable range of ale, both pump and bottled as well as a good wine list. The food is hearty and bold – snacks include home-made piccalilli and toast, chips and aioli, chicken wings, with full meals available too, and a dining room upstairs.

The Earl of Essex

25 Danbury Street N1 8LE
Telephone: 020 7424 5828
Monday: 3pm–11.30pm; Tuesday–Thursday: 12noon–11.30pm;
Friday & Saturday: 12noon–12.30am; Sunday: 12noon–11pm
Transport: Angel, Essex Road

Interesting and mostly successful blend of a US-style craft beer house and London pub, not just in décor but customers too, with a few old boys hanging on from earlier incarnations alongside the usual ageing youths and Islington professionals. A large wall chart indicates the day's beers at a point size that wouldn't challenge even Mr Magoo, and to further boost credentials they brew their own – evidence of which comes from the two hefty tanks taking up space behind the island bar. In fine weather, a pleasant garden provides a good amount of additional seating. Food is as Anglo-American as the rest: salt beef sandwich on rye, smoked BBQ ribs, and bringing it back home, the fish finger sandwich.

THE EARL OF ESSEX

KEG	HACKER	GOLD	LAGER	5.5%	PINT	£4.50	HALF	£2.00
KEG	RODENBACH	GRAND	CRU	6.8%	PINT	£6.50	HALF	£5.00
KEG	GREEN FLASH	BELGIAN		7.5%	PINT	£6.50	HALF	£3.50
KEG	SUMMER	WINE	WART HOG	6.9%	PINT	£5.50	HALF	£2.80
KEG	SLEEMANS	HONEY	BROWN	5.2%	PINT	£5.50	HALF	£2.80
KEG	STEENBRUGGE	WIT		5.0%	PINT	£5.00	HALF	£2.50
CASK	ART BREW	BABY	ANARCHIST	3.2%	PINT	£3.90	HALF	£2.00

BEER BOARD

CASK	MALLINSON	AMARILLO	4.2%	PINT	£3.90	HALF	£2.00
CASK	BURNING	SKY	PLATEAU	3.5%	PINT	£3.90	HALF	£2.00
CASK	HARBOUR	AMBER	4.0%	PINT	£4.00	HALF	£2.00
CASK	LILEYS	CIDER	4.5%	PINT	£4.00	HALF	£2.00
KEG	CAMDEN	HELLS	4.6%	PINT	£4.00	HALF	£2.00
KEG	GREEN FLASH	WIT	5.0%	PINT	£5.00	HALF	£2.50
CASK	CAMDEN	INK	STOUT	4.2%	PINT	£4.20	HALF	£2.00

The Greenwich Union

56 Royal Hill SE10 8RT
Telephone: 020 8692 6258
Monday-Friday: 12noon-11pm; Saturday: 11am-11pm;
Sunday: 11.30am-10.30pm
Transport: Greenwich

For those who complain that pubs are dark, smelly places, Greenwich's own Meantime brewery have stripped away all that and created something that's scrubbed, clean and wholesome; even the bar itself is pale wood where one might normally expect something more along the lines of deep mahogany. There's a conservatory with booth seating that opens directly on to a garden, which is all very light and pleasant though perhaps a little lacking in atmosphere. The beer is excellent, not just their own but a large range of bottles from overseas too.

The Harp

47 Chandos Place WC2N 4HS
Telephone: 020 7836 0291
Monday-Saturday: 10am-11pm; Sunday: 12noon-10.30pm
Transport: Charing Cross, Embankment

Small and almost always busy, there's little argument that The Harp has the West End's best-kept and widest variety of ale, cider and perry, without being overly beardy or serious about it. Food is limited to sausages served on baguette, as unpretentious a snack as one would expect from this genial place. There's a room upstairs if things get too busy, but even in a crush the downstairs is more appealing, with decorative stained glass windows at the front that open right across to reveal hanging baskets, and a rear entrance on Brydges Place, the narrowest alley in London.

King William IV

816 High Road E10 6AE
Telephone: 020 8556 2460
Monday-Thursday: 11am-12midnight;
Friday & Saturday: 11am-1am;
Sunday: 12noon-12midnight
Transport: 20, 48, 55, 56, 69, 97, 230,
257, 357, W15, W16, W19 buses

Right next to their brewery, this is Brodie's own pub, a huge place with a vast range of own-brewed beer. There's nothing subtle about it, it's big, loud and popular, managing to please beer snobs as well as those enticed by a cheap drink (just £2.50 a pint for Brodie's own) and a place to watch football. And then there may be one or two others led in this direction by the bar billiards, which is available in the back bar.

Old Coffee House

49 Beak Street W1F 9SF
Telephone: 020 7437 2197
Monday-Saturday: 11am-11pm; Sunday: 12noon-10.30pm
Transport: Oxford Circus, Piccadilly Circus

If Albert and Harold Steptoe had a pub, it might be like this: a room littered with old enamel signs and newer reproduction versions, a desiccated oil painting, taxidermy, old and defunct brewery mirrors and advertising (the sign above the bar dates from the Watney's Red Barrel era), and TVs at either end tuned to different sporting fixtures. For all this, the range of Brodie's beers is excellent, and the Coffee House's uncontrived, freewheeling scruffiness makes a pleasing contrast to some of its more obviously stylish neighbours.

WATCHMAKER TYDEMAN JEWELLERS

The Old Fountain

3 Baldwin Street EC1V 9NU
Telephone: 020 7253 2970
Daily: 11am-11pm
Transport: Old Street

There are plenty of prettier pubs, but few can rival the ale served here. It's an exceptional range and beautifully kept, small wonder then that this is a regular CAMRA award-winner. There are entrances on both Baldwin and Peerless Street, with the bar extending the full length even as it goes up a step, which gives the slight feeling of being in a corridor. An aquarium is an unlikely addition but not without charm, perhaps more welcome is a modest roof terrace. Family-run since the early 1960s, it's managed to move with the times while keeping a very distinctive character.

The Rake

14a Winchester Walk SE1 9AG
Telephone: 020 7407 0557
Monday-Friday: 12noon-11pm; Saturday: 10am-11pm;
Sunday: 12noon-8pm
Transport: London Bridge

Less a pub than it is a tasting area; it's a small and unlovely room that was formerly the small and unlovely Jubilee Café, but it's usually far too crowded for that to be noticeable, filled with customers eager to sample the vast range of bottled beers and rapidly changing barrels. An adjoining decked area significantly increases capacity.

Time for another?

Crown & Anchor

246 Brixton Road SW9 6AQ
Telephone: 020 7737 0060
Monday-Thursday: 4.30pm-12midnight;
Friday: 4.30pm-1am;
Saturday: 12noon-1am;
Sunday: 12noon-11pm
Transport: Brixton; Stockwell

The Elm Park Tavern

76 Elm Park SW2 2UB
Telephone: 07852 345 974
Monday-Friday: 4pm-12midnight;
Saturday: 12noon-12midnight;
Sunday: 12noon-11pm
Transport: 59, 109, 118, 133, 159,
250, 333 buses

The Grape & Grain

2 Anerley Hill SE19 2AA
Telephone: 020 8778 9688
Monday-Thursday: 12noon-11pm;
Friday & Saturday: 12noon-12midnight;
Sunday: 12noon-10.30pm
Transport: 157, 249, 358, 432 buses,
Crystal Palace

For the Guinness

There are those who claim that you can't get a decent pint of Guinness east of the Irish Sea. It's not one we'd care to make in any of the following.

Auld Shillelagh

105 Stoke Newington Church Street N16 0UD
Telephone: 020 7249 5951
Monday–Wednesday: 11am–11pm; Thursday–Saturday; 11am–1am;
Sunday: 12noon–12midnight
Transport: Stoke Newington

A cheerful place that some aficionados claim serves the capital's best Guinness. The staff certainly take the dark stuff seriously, delivering it to your table if you can't bear to wait at the bar for it to settle. The Auld Shillelagh appears miniscule from the street, but stretches far back with a beer garden at the rear. There's live music and theme nights, which can make for a grand night out but may limit conversation.

Cock & Bottle

17 Needham Road W11 2RP
Telephone: 020 7229 1550
Monday–Saturday: 12noon–11pm; Sunday: 12noon–10.30pm
Transport: Notting Hill Gate, Westbourne Park

A place for conversation and a quiet drink, and if that sounds like a minor selling point, you haven't set out in West London with such humble aims for some considerable time. There's nothing remotely fussy or contrived about this slightly shabby establishment that's run by an avuncular Irishman, whose portrait, in which he's surrounded Dali-style by hovering pints of Guinness, hangs on the wall. That they make a fiery Bloody Mary, the beer is good and the Guinness excellent is quite recommendation enough.

Whittington & Cat

26 Highgate Hill N19 5NL
Telephone: 020 7272 3274
Monday-Friday: 11am-11pm
Transport: Archway

A resolutely traditional Irish pub, it could hardly be more welcoming and is a reminder that there was much to enjoy even before sharing plates and craft ale. Take a seat on a squashy banquette, sip a pint of Guinness with a bag of Tayto cheese and onion, study the rows of darts trophies above the bar, ornamental figurines of cats and horses, net curtains over the window and the disconcerting lingering smell of cigarettes, six years after the smoking ban. A small group of regulars chat at the bar, and no one pays attention to the much-repaired case containing the preserved remains of a cat, presumably an homage to the pub's name.

On the dark side

The Kensington Park

139 Ladbroke Grove W10 6HJ
Telephone: 020 7727 5876
Sunday-Thursday: 10am-11pm;
Friday & Saturday: 10am-12midnight
Transport: Ladbroke Grove

The Toucan

19 Carlisle Street W1D 3BY
Telephone: 020 7437 4123
Monday-Saturday: 11am-11pm;
Sunday: 4.30pm-10.30pm
Transport: Tottenham Court Road

When you're planning a party

Rooms for hire in central locations, just add friends.

The Constitution

42 St Pancras Way NW1 0QT
Telephone: 020 7387 4805
Monday-Wednesday: 11am-12midnight;
Thursday-Saturday: 11am-1am;
Sunday: 11am-10.30pm
Transport: Camden Road, Camden Town

When their cellar bar's not being used for one of the regular jazz or club nights, it's an ideal party venue with low ceilings, its own bar and stage. If things get too hot, the back doors open on to Regent's Canal. Upstairs it's very much a local's place, with the pool table seeing plenty of action and a large, attractive terrace that overlooks the canal.

The Edgar Wallace

40 Essex Street WC2R 3JE
Telephone: 020 7353 3120
Monday-Friday: 11am-11pm
Transport: Temple

Decorated with old ads and point-of-sale material for beer, cigarettes, shoes and soft drinks that make it look rather more like a Brighton second-hand shop than a pub frequented by hacks escaping the Royal Courts of Justice over the road, this was once a favourite establishment of its namesake mystery writer. Not that it matters much; the ale is excellent, there's good, unchallenging food and an upstairs room with its own bar can be hired for events.

The Golden Lion

5 King Street SW1Y 6QY
Telephone: 020 7925 0007
Monday-Friday: 11am-11pm; Saturday: 12noon-5pm
Transport: Green Park, Piccadilly Circus

Attractive bow-fronted exterior with decorative glass and a woody interior that has some unexpected flourishes, it seems either deathly quiet or madly busy depending on the time of day – after work it's thronged with staff from Christie's and other nearby galleries. There's a nice upstairs room that's available for hire, with windows looking on to King Street.

The Queen's Head

5 Denman Street W1D 7HN
Telephone: 020 7437 1540
Monday-Thursday: 11am-11.30pm;
Friday & Saturday: 11am-12midnight;
Sunday: 12noon-10.30pm
Transport: Piccadilly Circus

A plain and traditionally-outfitted upstairs room with a separate entrance and its own bar is just part of the appeal of this remarkable find that's barely a minute from Piccadilly Circus. There's also a good selection of cask and bottled ale, decent food, attractive etched mirrors and original carved wood features, only a rather heavy band with the decorating mars it a little – but barely.

The Wheatsheaf

25 Rathbone Place W1T 1JB
Telephone: 020 7580 1585
Monday-Friday: 11.30am-11pm; Saturday: 12noon-11pm
Transport: Goodge Street, Tottenham Court Road

Once a favourite with Fitzrovia's literary set, it's now nine-to-fivers who keep the tills ringing in this mock-Tudor oddity north of Oxford Street. Long and narrow, with leaded stained glass windows and the unfortunate addition of a TV, it's not the maddest of the city's Tudoresque pubs (that gong should probably go to the towering Three Greyhounds on Greek Street), but eccentric enough. The upstairs function room is used for comedy and literary events, and as a popular venue for leaving parties it has been the site of countless teary recriminations.

Keeping it going

Calthorpe Arms

252 Grays Inn Road WC1X 8JR
Telephone: 020 7278 4732
Monday-Saturday: 11am-11.30pm;
Sunday: 12noon-10.30pm
Transport: King's Cross, Russell Square

Crown Tavern

43 Clerkenwell Green EC1R 0EG
Telephone: 020 7253 4973
Daily: 12noon-12midnight
Transport: Farringdon

The George

213 Strand WC2R 1AP
Telephone: 020 7353 9638
Monday-Saturday: 11am-12midnight
Sunday: 12noon-9pm
Transport: Temple

The Old Crown

33 New Oxford Street WC1A 1BH
Telephone: 020 7836 9121
Sunday-Wednesday: 12noon-12midnight
Thursday-Saturday: 12noon-3am;
Sunday 12noon-12midnight
Transport: Holborn,
Tottenham Court Road

Because there's nowhere you'd rather be

One shouldn't play favourites, so let's just say that this is where we're heading when the lights go out.

The Coach & Horses

29 Greek Street W1D 5DH
Telephone: 020 7437 5920
Monday–Thursday: 11am–11.30pm;
Friday & Saturday: 11am–12midnight;
Sunday: 12noon–10.30pm
Transport: Leicester Square

Perhaps Soho's most famous hostelry, it remains a favourite
of locals as well as visitors eager to see where Jeffrey Bernard,
Francis Bacon and other West End notables and undesirables
spent so much of their time. Its interior is unpretentious, a
pleasing blend of wood and red Formica, with authentic
1970s touches. It is perhaps at its best on Sundays; during
the day it's peaceful and quiet, come the evening a cheerful
sing-along begins.

The Cross Keys

31 Endell Street WC2H 9EB
Telephone: 0207 836 5185
Monday–Saturday: 11am–11pm; Sunday: 12noon–10.30pm
Transport: Covent Garden

Easily spotted by a proud display of foliage and drinkers spilling
in to the street, its exterior charm is considerable, but it's
even better inside. Among the most dimly-lit pubs we know,
rose-coloured lightbulbs provide a warm glow and just enough
light to make out the eccentric assemblage hanging from walls
and ceiling: copper pots and kettles, an old diver's helmet,
photographs and paintings. A homely, comfortable place with
friendly bar staff and Brodie's excellent ales, it feels a long way
from the madness of Covent Garden, just a few feet away.

The Blue Posts

22 Berwick Street W1F 0QA
Telephone: 020 7437 5008
Monday-Friday: 11.30am-11pm; Saturday: 12noon-11pm
Transport: Oxford Circus

A blissfully unremarkable corner pub – even the name
is commonplace, there are two more Blue Posts in Soho
alone – it is still frequented by market traders from nearby
Berwick Street, film and music business hustlers and
strivers, and the occasional weary tourist. It has the worn-
in living room atmosphere familiar from the years before
leather sofas and artfully mismatched armchairs took hold.
Service is brisk, eavesdropping can be rewarding. For a
quiet mid-afternoon reviver, it's all you can ask for.

The Jolly Butchers

204 Stoke Newington High Street N16 7HU
Telephone: 020 7249 9471
Monday-Thursday: 4pm-12midnight; Friday: 4pm-1am;
Saturday: 12noon-1am; Sunday: 12noon-11pm
Transport: Stoke Newington

Justifiably popular, it combines a large and excellent
cider and ale selection (including a great many hard-
to-find bottles) with hearty food and a companionable
environment. In common with other properties that are
now revived after years of neglect, the interior is not much
to look at, but there is wonderful ironwork over the window
exteriors, albeit under rather too many layers of paint.

The Lord Clyde

27 Clennam Street SE1 1ER
Telephone: 020 7407 3397
Monday-Friday: 11am-11pm; Saturday: 12noon-11pm;
Sunday: 12noon-6pm
Transport: Borough

Rome has its fountains that emerge from a tangle of tiny streets, London has The Lord Clyde, tucked away in the backstreets of Borough revealing its magnificent frontage only to the intrepid traveller. The current pub dates from 1913, decked out in Truman's cream and green livery, with an eagle standing proud. Inside it's sparer than might be expected, albeit with some decorative mirrors and heavy curtains on brass rails over the two doors. It has a good ale selection, simple food and a cheerful, welcoming atmosphere, as one might hope from an establishment that's been run by the same family for more than 50 years.

The Newman Arms

23 Rathbone Street W1T 1NG
Telephone: 020 7636 1127
Monday-Friday: 12noon-11.30pm
Transport: Goodge Street, Tottenham Court Road, Warren Street

A refuge in the West End, family-run but not for families – it's 18 and over in the bar. A place to meet friends or read a book in an atmosphere less frenetic than that which surrounds it. The upstairs Pie Room is an ideal place to bring overseas visitors desiring traditional British décor and sustenance in the form not of just of pies but savoury and sweet puddings too. The Pie Room can be reached by its own entrance on Newman Passage, a street notorious as the site of the first murder in Michael Powell's 1960 film, *Peeping Tom*.

Ye Olde Mitre

1 Ely Court EC1N 6SJ
Telephone: 020 7405 4751
Monday-Friday: 11am-11pm
Transport: Chancery Lane, Farringdon

Accessed by discreet doorway-sized gaps in either Ely
Place or Hatton Garden, on first visiting it can be quite a
surprise that so many other people have found their way
to this hidden little place. Perhaps after close to 500 years
the secret is out. Built in 1546 by the Bishop of Ely for the
use of his servants, and used as a prison and hospital during
the Civil War, the dark wood-panelled walls and carved
high-backed chairs give a slight ecclesiastical atmosphere.
But it's matters secular that current habitués discuss, many
of them from the nearby offices of BT and Sainsbury's.

Prince George

40 Parkholme Road E8 3AG
Telephone: 020 7254 6060
Monday-Thursday: 5pm-12midnight; Friday: 5pm-1am;
Saturday: 2pm-1am; Sunday: 2pm-10.30pm
Transport: Dalston Junction, Hackney Central

A stately old pub that has done a grand job of rolling with
seismic demographic shifts in the neighbourhood. Wooden
bar, stools, benches and floor bear the marks of many years'
use, not battered but comfortably worn-in. Posters and an
enormous world map are handy fallbacks if conversation
lags, and the ale selection should keep all but the most fussy
happy. One caveat: arrive at nine on a Saturday night when
it's at it busiest and it may be that there's nowhere you'd less
like to be, but on a quiet weekday it's just about perfect.

The Royal Oak

44 Tabard Street SE1 4JU
Telephone: 020 7357 7173
Monday-Friday: 11am-11.30pm; Saturday: 12noon-11.30pm;
Sunday: 12noon-9pm
Transport: Borough

An attractive modest corner pub, it has the large central bar connecting the two main bars, and a third between them that's just a standing area with a serving hatch. With no music, no video games, no fruit machines, just a faint old-dog aroma, here is somewhere to enjoy good conversation and excellent beer from this establishment's Sussex owners, Harvey's. There's food, too, of a traditional and hearty type, which is just as well. This is the sort of comfortable place where one drink inevitably leads to another.

The Shakespeare

57 Allen Road N16 8RY
Telephone: 020 7254 4190
Monday-Thursday: 5pm-12midnight; Friday: 5pm-1am;
Saturday: 12noon-1am; Sunday: 12noon-10.30pm
Transport: Canonbury, Dalston Kingsland

Sometimes it's the little things that make all the difference, in this case a pretty fireplace with leather club fender on which to warm yourself, but perhaps only briefly. Others may enjoy that you can order a pizza from La Barca next door and eat it here. Then there's the garden and the seating out on the street. The remnants of etched glass and dark wood. Or what looks very much like the figurehead from a ship. It's indefinable, but whatever it is, The Shakespeare has it.

The Southampton Arms

139 Highgate Road NW5 1LE
Daily: 12noon–11pm/12midnight (depending on how busy they are)
Transport: Gospel Oak, Kentish Town

At the beginning of 2010 a grotty and unloved little pub with fake stained glass windows, huge TV and decaying custom was taken over and transformed. Everything extraneous was removed leaving only a fireplace, simple wooden furniture, small garden and a dog. Behind the bar things were streamlined too: they now offer ale, cider and meat. Neither of the first two from large operations and frequently rotated; the latter comprising scotch eggs, pork pies and pork rolls. It is a simple formula executed with love and care. It can sometimes get uncomfortably busy – its proximity to Hampstead Heath doesn't help – but persistence usually rewards with a seat. In keeping with the minimal approach, cards are not accepted.

The Three Kings

7 Clerkenwell Close EC1R 0DY
Telephone: 020 7253 0483
Monday–Friday: 12noon–11pm; Saturday: 5.30pm–11pm
Transport: Farringdon

There is rock and roll in this pub's genes. Landlord John Eichler decamped here from the fabled Hope & Anchor on Upper Street, Islington, carving out an unconventional niche in a corner of the city that has long been associated with dissenters. Nowadays John's son Deke is in charge, catering to a truly mixed group of patrons, many of whom have been regulars since a time when the vinyl jukebox wasn't a novelty. It is cheerfully ramshackle, with outlandish décor (the rhino head is unmissable), quiz nights and an air of bonhomie.

Acknowledgements

Thank you to the following people for advice, tips and companionship on this most arduous task: Sam Blunden, Nick Brown, PJ Crittenden, Ian Johnsen, Alex Lim, Lindy Loo McDonnell, Jon Martin, Tim Matthews, Teri Olins, Iain Pitchford, Bob Stanley and the many publicans who are keeping these institutions alive.

We studied numerous books in our research, most notable among them *The New London Spy* (Hunter Davies; Anthony Blond, 1966), *Nairn's London* (Ian Nairn; Penguin, 1967), *Soho Night & Day* (Frank Norman; Martin Secker & Warburg, 1966), *London Pubs* (Alan Reeve-Jones; Batsford, 1962) and *The Good Pub Guide* (Alisdair Aird and Fiona Stapley; Ebury, 2013). londonist.com added greatly to our long working list of pubs to visit, while the unvarnished opinions shared on beerintheevening.com did much to reduce it.

A-Z of pubs

Index of pubs by postcode